THE WILD WILD WEST

The Wild Wild West

Pioneering the Decentralized World of Web3

TUDAMOON

Carl Loser

Tudamoon Publishing

CONTENTS

ABOUT COVER ILLUSTRATION

The illustrations on the cover of the book was made by Midjourney AI. The prompts were engineered by Tudamoon. The placement of the text and putting it all together was also completed by Tudamoon.

Tudamoon was inspired by the famous painting *Wanderer above the Sea of Fog* by Caspar David Friedrich.

When considering the back cover illustration, Tudamoon had the Wanderer from the Wanderer above the Sea of Fog in mind, but instead of looking towards the obstacles ahead with the wanderer's back towards the viewer's perspective, Tudamoon decided to depict a Cowboy with a background from the American Wild West to represent a time period of the past.

For the front cover illustration, Wanderer from the Wanderer above the Sea of Fog was also in mind, this time Tudamoon decided to keep the perspective the same as the famous painting, but changing the theme to a new technological, overwhelming, busy looking world. So much going on, yet the pioneers journey has just begun.

ISBN: 978-0-9980407-3-8 (Paperback)
ISBN: 978-0-9980407-4-5 (Ebook)
ISBN: 978-0-9980407-5-2 (Audiobook)

Library of Congress Control Number: 2024900206

Names, characters, and places are products of the author's perspective and may not reflect another person's truth and/or perspective. This book was made to the best of the author's knowledge of historical events, concepts and more. It is suggested to always do your own research.

The content of this book is provided for informational & entertainment purposes only and does not constitute financial, legal, or professional advice. The reader should not rely on any material in this book as a basis for making any business, legal or financial decisions and is advised to consult a qualified professional for specific advice tailored to their situation. The author and publisher expressly disclaim any liability for any loss or damage that may arise from the use or reliance on information contained in this book.

First Edition, 2024

Dedication

This book is dedicated to my wife, Mallory. This would not have been possible without her unconditional support and love. I am forever thankful.

In Memory of

In Memory of Bananas who was an amazing friend and all-around great person who had an enormous impact on my life and my experience in pioneering web3. He left this realm after 32 years. Life should not be taken for granted - thank you for the reminder. Memento Mori. Love you bro!

Honorable Mentions

I would also like to thank all my family and friends for their support. It's shaped me to be who I am today.
I also appreciate my adversaries who have challenged me giving me the motivation to compete and do better.

| 1 |

Introduction

The path to decentralization began for me in 2013 when I first became interested in politics. I was highly interested in limiting government because I felt the system was broken. Since that time, I fell in love with the concept of decentralization, even though I hadn't specifically thought of using the term "decentralization." I have always enjoyed giving more power to the individual and property rights. With that being said, I am forever thankful for the Mises Institute which gave me free access to books to read and audiobooks to listen to. My favorite economist whose works they feature is Murray Rothbard. Rothbard was very much in favor of a free market and what the free market can offer. This journey has guided me to where I stand today.

In 2016, I was first introduced to the term "decentralization" shortly after my initial investment in Bitcoin. The idea of Bitcoin derived from decentralizing the control of fiat money. This essentially involves trying to put an end to centralized control over the money supply, transactions, and custody. The most remarkable aspect of this movement and idea is that it didn't require force for people to embrace it. The free market enabled Bitcoin and subsequent cryptocurrencies to compete with central bank-issued fiat money (notes). In line with true capitalist principles, the belief is to outdo bad ideas with better ones. Let the best competitor prevail and the market make its choice. This approach embodies the essence of a truly free society.

Decentralization involves spreading out decision-making, planning, services, processes, and authority from a concentrated group within an organization to a broader range of individuals who have a stake or interest in the subject matter. On the other hand, Centralization refers to an organizational or systemic structure where all decision-making powers and authority are concentrated in a single point or location, typically at the highest level of the organization or system. In this model, decisions, directives, and policies are made by a central body or a few individuals at the top, and these are then passed down through the hierarchy to be implemented at lower levels. This might seem overwhelming at this moment, but I'm confident that by the end of this book, you'll have a much clearer understanding of everything discussed.

You might wonder why a book exploring themes of cryptocurrency, decentralization, and power dynamics bears the title "The Wild Wild West." It's a valid question, and the answer is straightforward. The term "Wild Wild West" is often used to describe the world of web3 because of its striking similarities to the historical frontier. While it's commonly said that history repeats itself, I prefer to think that history rhymes. By the end of this book, the reason for its title will become overwhelmingly clear.

In this book, we will embark on a journey through the realm of pure decentralization, engaging with its ongoing conflict against the forces of centralization. This narrative isn't framed as a battle between good and evil; rather, it's a deep dive into the natural ebb and flow of power dynamics. Alongside this, there's a detailed exploration of the World Wide Web's evolution, a crucial development often taken for granted in our everyday life. Taking a step back to understand this evolution can offer us invaluable insights.

As we lay down these foundational concepts, the book then shifts into a more captivating phase. Here, I draw thought-provoking parallels between the characters in the web3 eco-system and the diverse, iconic personas from the Wild West. The resemblance between these modern digital figures and their historical Wild West counterparts is both striking and insightful. Adding a personal touch, I will share my own experiences, offering a window into the life of a web3 pioneer, navigating this new digital frontier.

To conclude the book, the focus turns to what I believe is the ideal state of power balance for fostering optimal prosperity. Here, we'll explore how balanced power dynamics can be the key to success and growth, not just in the digital realm, but in all aspects of life. It aims to provide insights into achieving a harmonious balance that benefits everyone, bridging the gap between the digital future and our current realities.

In the digital age, the internet has evolved into an infinite tapestry, woven with endless threads of information, communication, and interaction, all available at the mere tap of a finger. Despite its years of existence, we continue to chart new territories within this vast expanse. Our journey begins into the uncharted territories of the internet, a place as vast and untamed as the West once was. So, in the lyrics of Tupac Shakur, "now let me welcome everybody to the wild, wild west."

| 2 |

Understanding Decentralization

The Wild West Comparison

The Wild West, spanning the late 19th century in the United States, represents a time of exploration, settlement, and the quest for prosperity. The territories west of the Mississippi River were untamed and, in many respects, lawless, defined by vast landscapes that presented both vast opportunities and immense challenges. In the absence of centralized infrastructure and governance, order, economics, and social norms often arose organically, molded by the eclectic mix of people who ventured there.

In this decentralized landscape, communities often had to self-govern. Without a strong central authority, they would come together to create their own provisional governments, form local committees, or rely on respected community figures to make decisions and arbitrate disputes. Law and order, such an essential bedrock of society, found its keepers in vigilantes or local sheriffs. These individuals would step in to fill the void left by the distant or non-existent formal law enforcement, dispensing justice in ways that sometimes aligned with community interests and at other times veered towards personal vendettas.

The economic heartbeat of the Wild West was unlike anything seen in more developed parts of the country. In the absence of structured banks or financial establishments, trade often thrived on barter systems or hinged on tangible assets like gold. This gave immense power and influence to miners, farmers, and ranchers, who became de facto determinants of local economic health. The channels of communication were yet another aspect dictated by the sprawling nature of the territories. Without organized postal services, messages relied on the bravery and endurance of individual riders, such as those in the iconic Pony Express. News and rumors, in the absence of official channels, would often circulate through saloons, campfires, and informal gatherings.

But as time wore on, the waves of centralization began to reshape the Wild West. The U.S. government began to stake its claim, establishing territories, and later integrating them as states, ushering in a more structured legal and administrative canvas. Entities like the Texas Rangers came into existence, symbolizing a more standardized approach to law enforcement and reducing the need for local, makeshift justice. The economic structures saw transformation with the arrival of banks and financial institutions, and the telegraph brought about a revolution in communication, bringing distant parts of the country closer. Perhaps the most symbolic transition from decentralization to centralization was the completion of the Transcontinental Railroad in 1869. While it made travel and trade more efficient, it also signified the unifying of a nation, bridging its decentralized past with a centralized vision for the future.

The Wild West, with its decentralized spirit of independence and self-reliance, slowly melded into the larger centralized frameworks of the burgeoning United States. The roles once taken up by pioneers, either by choice or necessity, found themselves integrated into more formalized structures, marking the end of one of the most iconic eras of American history.

The Background and History

The real wild west was a conquest that lasted a period of around 150 years sending pioneers from the east coast of America all the way to the West Coast. The frontier started in the 1750s and ended around 1890. The pioneers entering the new world were essentially on their own in the unexplored world. There were rules and laws, but there was not a means of centralized enforcement. Decentralization was the way of life in the Wild, Wild West.

During this time, pioneers would eventually find a place they would call home. These pioneers were very aware of power and what it took to survive. Guns leveled the playing field of power. Typically, one person with a gun was no more powerful than another with a gun. Pioneers understood this and it then became a numbers game. Strength by numbers. Pioneers would form alliances and settlements and protect each other from all types of conflicts, especially outlaws. As new conflicts arisen, so did more rules. Eventually this led to full centralization. Many people compare the Wild, Wild West to the Web3 movement.

The World Wide Web has seen the full cycle of power. The first version of the World Wide Web will be referred to as "Web 1.0." Web 1.0 was during the time of pioneers and exploration of the internet. Web 1.0 began in the late 1990s. During this time, the web was primarily used to access and share static information, such as text and images. Web 1.0 was characterized using simple HTML pages and the absence of interactive or dynamic features. Websites were typically one-way sources of information, and users were unable to interact with them or contribute their own content.

The exploration continued leading to "Web 2.0" or "Web2" which is where the web became more interactive and user-driven, with the introduction of social media, user-generated content, and other dynamic features. Web2 was characterized using web-based applications and services, as well as the ability for users to interact with and contribute to websites. This marked a significant shift from the static and one-way nature of the web in the early days of Web 1.0. Web 2.0 has paved the way for the current state of the web, which is increasingly social, interactive, and personalized.

During the early days of the web, companies gained power by providing access to information and services that were previously not available online. As the web grew and evolved into web2, companies continued to gain power by providing platforms and services that allowed users to interact with each other and share information and content. This gave companies the ability to collect and analyze vast amounts of data about users and their behavior, which they could then use to target advertising and other services more effectively. Additionally, the rise of social media and other web-based services gave companies the ability to reach large audiences and shape public opinion in ways that were not previously possible. This, in turn, gave companies significant influence over the online environment and the flow of information on the web.

These companies have been criticized for exploiting their power in various ways. For example, some web2 companies have been accused of using their dominance of the online environment to stifle competition and maintain their market share. This can lead to higher prices and less choice for consumers. Additionally, the collection and analysis of vast amounts of user data by web2 companies has raised concerns about privacy and the potential for this information to be used for malicious purposes. Finally, the ability of web2 companies to shape public opinion and control the flow of information online has led to concerns about the potential for manipulation and the distortion of the truth.

Currently as it is playing out, numerous large-scale web2 corporations exercise their influence by utilizing users' data through sophisticated marketing strategies and even selling private information. This concentration of personal data not only raises ethical concerns but also makes these entities prime targets for cyber-attacks. Despite these risks, many users continue to place their trust in these companies. Unfortunately, this trust is often betrayed through data breaches, highlighting the perils of relying on third parties for data security.

Initially, it was logical for internet users to entrust their data to companies, primarily because these organizations boasted superior security measures compared to the average user. But as internet users become savvier and adept in cybersecurity practices, a shift is occurring. Many are now seeking to reclaim control over their data through the concept of decentralization. We call this movement of decentralization, "Web3."

The Web3 movement is a fascinating and multifaceted revolution, embodying principles like ownership of data, digital property rights (including digital intellectual property), decentralized finance, and decentralized currency, among others. At its core, decentralization is the guiding principle, and it's made possible through several groundbreaking technologies and systems.

Key among these are decentralized networks, which allow for the distribution of data across multiple nodes, eliminating the need for a central server. This approach significantly enhances security and resilience against attacks or failures. Decentralized protocols play a crucial role too, establishing the rules and standards for data transmission and interaction in a way that's not controlled by any single entity.

Then there's the backbone of Web3, decentralized blockchains. These digital ledgers record transactions across many computers so that the record cannot be altered retroactively without the alteration of all subsequent blocks and the consensus of the network. This technology is fundamental to cryptocurrencies and ensures transparency and security in a decentralized manner.

Lastly, decentralized governance systems, particularly Decentralized Autonomous Organizations (DAOs), represent a
radical shift in organizational structure and control. DAOs are
governed by their members collectively, based on a set of rules
enforced on the blockchain. They operate without centralized
leadership, making decisions through member consensus, which
can lead to more democratic and equitable outcomes.

These revolutionary technologies are at the forefront of the
Web3 movement, paving the way for a more decentralized,
secure, and user-empowered internet. The implications of these
technologies are vast, potentially reshaping everything from online interactions and financial transactions to how we perceive
and assert ownership in the digital realm.

Anarchy

To truly grasp the concept of decentralization, it's essential
to explore its most extreme form. Think of it like anarchy.
Many people think of anarchy as protesters throwing Molotov
Cocktails at government buildings. How I look at the meaning
of anarchy is by breaking the word down. "An" is the lack of or
none of, while "Archy" means rule or ruler. So, anarchy literally
means the lack of rulers. Therefore, when someone says they
are anarchist, in a sense they are someone who believes in no
ruling power, no system, and no hierARCHIES. Most people
relate anarchy to chaos which can be true. However, what most
people fail to see is that nature organically brings order.

Hierarchies are indeed a natural and inescapable aspect of
life. Just as some people are naturally taller, faster, or stronger

than others, nature operates under its own set of unyielding laws and principles. These inherent truths and principles create diversity and difference in the world around us. They are the unchangeable facets of our reality, shaping everything from the physical attributes of individuals to the broader dynamics of ecosystems. This natural order, with its inherent hierarchies, is a fundamental part of the world we live in.

The concept of natural law is a profound philosophical idea, positing that certain laws are intrinsic to nature, universal, and timeless. This theory is grounded in the belief that there exists a moral order in the universe, one that is independent of human-made laws and institutions. According to natural law theory, the moral principles guiding human behavior are derived from the very nature of human beings and the world around us, making them applicable across all cultures and societies.

Proponents of natural law argue that it offers a universal moral framework, a standard against which the fairness and justice of human laws and institutions can be measured. This perspective has significantly influenced the development of legal and moral systems throughout history and continues to spark debate in philosophical and political circles.

The relationship between natural law and morality is intricate. One way to understand their interplay is to see natural law as providing a foundational moral framework or set of principles. These principles serve as a benchmark for evaluating the moral substance of human laws and actions. In this context, natural law is seen as a standard of moral excellence, a yardstick for assessing the fairness, justice, and goodness of human laws and institutions.

Concurrently, morality acts as a guide for individual behavior, aligning actions with the inherent moral order of the universe as dictated by natural law. In this sense, natural law and morality are complementary: natural law offers a broad framework for moral judgment, while morality offers specific guidance for individual conduct within this framework. This integration of natural law and morality creates a cohesive system for understanding and navigating the moral dimensions of human life.

In my view, anarchy is not just a theoretical concept but a tangible reality, often overlooked in the modern world. Contrary to popular belief, anarchy exists in any space where societal rules are not actively enforced, and it's the individual's moral compass that guides behavior. In such scenarios, the absence of law enforcement leaves people to act on their personal sense of right and wrong. I see examples of anarchy in remote areas like the middle of the woods where no enforcement of the law exists or within groups that choose to operate outside the established legal framework.

I believe that anarchy, a blend of natural law and human morals, can maintain order, especially in smaller groups. However, as these groups grow, disruptive elements often lead to the establishment of rules and the formation of basic governance structures. This progression, driven by conflict and the need for order, gradually leads to more centralized and powerful entities, and eventually, to Totalitarian and revolution.

From my perspective, this cycle starts with anarchy and moves towards centralization, influenced by natural law and human nature. While every nation begins in an anarchic state, either from revolution or a breakdown in law and order, this phase is often fleeting and unnoticed, particularly in rapidly growing populations.

Totalitarianism

To fully understand the concept of decentralization, we must understand its polar opposite, Totalitarianism. Totalitarianism is the extreme form of centralization. This is a topic many of you might have encountered in your government classes. History is full of examples of Totalitarian governments, but for a centralized entity to reach this stage, it often requires a complex mix of propaganda and manipulation to convince people to support the centralized power. Individuals may also be drawn in due to coercion or the presence of immediate danger.

Without the use of propaganda, coercion, or the threat of imminent danger, the likelihood of people supporting a corrupt centralized power significantly diminishes. Dissatisfaction and conflicting values with the centralized entity can lead to a faster onset of revolution or uprising. Therefore, maintaining the illusion becomes crucial for the centralized power to keep its constituents supportive.

This dynamic between the people and the centralized authority is a delicate balance. The art of persuasion and control plays a critical role in sustaining a tyrannical regime. It's a stark reminder of the power of narrative and the importance of critical thinking in any society. Understanding this extreme form of centralization helps in appreciating the value and potential of decentralization, where power is more evenly distributed and less susceptible to the corrupting influence of absolute control.

As we discuss further, my focus will be on the cycle of power and control, particularly the transition from decentralized to centralized systems and vice versa. In my perspective, anarchy represents the ultimate form of decentralization, standing in absolute contrast to Totalitarian, which I see as the extreme of centralization. This viewpoint provides a unique perspective through which to examine the evolution of societies and the perpetual cycles of power and governance.

I believe that understanding this dynamic is crucial. It sheds light on how societies transform and evolve, often swinging between these two extremes. By examining anarchy and Totalitarian as endpoints of a spectrum, we gain insights into the forces that drive societal change and the challenges that come with different forms of governance. This exploration is not just an academic exercise; it's a journey into understanding the very fabric of human society and the complex interplay of power and control that shapes our world.

Decentralization

Decentralization is a powerful response to the limitations and failings of centralized systems. It's the story of how inefficiencies, eroded trust, and obsolescence in centralized structures have repeatedly given rise to a decentralized approach, reshaping the socio-economic, technological, and political landscapes throughout history.

Decentralization is what happens when common people get fed up with the "big guys at the top" not getting things right. When the centralized entities in charge start dropping the ball, getting all tangled up in red tape, or just seem out of touch, decentralization starts to ponder in people's heads as a good option. Decentralization can happen immediately or over a period of time. However, typically centralization takes place over a period of time exponentially.

The internet fundamentally democratized information access, challenging the once nearly invincible dominance of centralized media. This is decentralization in action, breaking down barriers and redistributing power.

But why does decentralization gain traction? Often, it's when centralized entities, governments, or corporate giants, get bogged down in their own bureaucracy. They become slow, unresponsive dinosaurs, unable to adapt to the rapidly changing needs of the people they serve. Add to this mix a dash of corruption or controversy, and you have a recipe for a public that's hungry for transparency, accountability, and a more localized approach.

Socio-political movements, often rooted in grassroots activism or desires for regional autonomy, also lean towards decentralization. They typically emerge in response to the perceived overreach or ineffectiveness of centralized authorities. Moreover, centralized systems are inherently vulnerable to large-scale collapses, especially when faced with significant disruptions like natural or human-made disasters.

Now, let's break down centralization versus decentralization in a less formal way. Centralization is like having one big boss who calls all the shots. It can be neat and efficient, sure, but it can also get rigid and out of touch. As for Decentralization, that's more like a bunch of smaller teams calling their own shots.

It's closer to action, more creative, and it gives people a real say in what's going on. It's about "spreading the love" or in this case, distributing power. Thus, making sure everyone gets a piece of the action.

In a centralized organization, information and tasks flow upwards, leading to decisions made at the top. This can work well, but it can also lead to a disconnect from the realities on the ground. In contrast, a decentralized organization is a hive of activity, where anyone spotting a problem can rally a team, propose a solution, and have it assessed by the wider network. It's dynamic, agile, and innovative. It still comes with challenges. Maintaining consistency and having a unified direction can be tough.

The dance between centralization and decentralization is a tale of power, adaptability, and the relentless pursuit of efficiency and innovation. As we navigate this ever-changing landscape, the interplay between these two approaches continues to shape our world in profound ways. The pursuit of decentralization is evident in numerous areas, with some achieving successful decentralization while others continue to experience an ongoing struggle between centralization and decentralization.

| 3 |

Real Instances of Decentralization

In today's rapidly evolving digital realm, the concept of decentralization is gaining unprecedented momentum, reshaping everything from socio-political movements to the very way we interact with technology and manage our finances. This shift towards a more distributed, less centralized world is vividly illustrated through various examples, each highlighting the transformative power of decentralization.

The Zapatista Uprising: A Decentralized Revolution

The Zapatista uprising in the Lacandon Jungle of Chiapas, Mexico, which began in 1994, stands as a compelling example of how decentralization can be harnessed in socio-political movements. Named after Emiliano Zapata, a key figure in the

Mexican Revolution, the Zapatista movement is remarkable for its structure: decentralized, fluid, and deeply democratic.

At the heart of the Zapatista movement were primarily indigenous people, rising against the Mexican government's marginalization and neglect. Unlike many movements, they didn't rally around a single charismatic leader. Instead, they operated through a network of autonomous communities, each making decisions through local councils. This structure was a deliberate choice, reflecting their ideology that emphasized collective action and local governance over centralized authority.

This decentralized approach enabled the Zapatistas to mobilize swiftly, adapt to evolving situations, and build a resilient movement that couldn't be easily quashed by targeting a few leaders. It's a modern-day David versus Goliath tale, with David refusing to adhere to the traditional rules of engagement.

The Zapatistas challenge conventional notions of leadership and organization. In a world fixated on individual heroes or leaders, they demonstrate the strength of leaderless movements. They exemplify that sometimes, the most potent force for change is not a singular voice but a community united by a common vision.

Their struggle transcends a mere fight for rights or land; it's about re-envisioning societal organization, about how people can exercise collective power without sacrificing individual voices. In an era increasingly skeptical of top-down leadership models, the Zapatista movement is a model for future decentralized socio-political movements.

Today, as we face complex global challenges and interconnected issues, the lessons from the Zapatista uprising resonate more than ever. They share the importance of resilience, the effectiveness of decentralized networks, and the enduring power of grassroots movements.

Netflix: An Entertainment Decentralized Revolution

The dynamic between centralization and decentralization is a recurring theme across various societal aspects, including the evolution of media consumption, particularly in the context of American television viewing.

In the early days of television, the experience was relatively centralized. Families gathered around their TV sets, equipped with antennas that captured a limited number of channels. This setup created a collective viewership experience, where most people watched the same handful of shows. Television, in this era, was a unifying medium, bringing diverse audiences together for shared viewing experiences.

The advent of cable TV initially seemed to decentralize this experience by offering a broader variety of channels and content. However, over time, cable television became dominated by a few large corporations. These entities controlled everything from channel lineups to subscription pricing, effectively recentralizing what was initially a step towards decentralization. Moreover, cable TV imposed strict viewing schedules, limiting the freedom of choice for viewers.

Netflix enters the market which is a game-changer in the media landscape. Initially offering DVDs by mail, Netflix enabled viewers to watch movies at their convenience, breaking away from the rigid schedules of cable TV. This service evolved into a streaming model, offering an à la carte viewing experience. This shift further decentralized media consumption, empowering viewers with greater control over what, when, and how they watched content.

However, this decentralization brought about a fragmented landscape. Exclusive content became tied to specific streaming services, requiring viewers to subscribe to multiple platforms to access a wide range of shows and movies. While streaming services offer more choice, they also pose the risk of re-centralization. If a few streaming giants were to dominate the market, we could see a return to a more centralized system.

Moreover, the cost factor plays a significant role. The cumulative expense of subscribing to multiple streaming services can exceed traditional cable costs, posing a challenge for consumers who wish to access a comprehensive range of content without paying a premium. This situation highlights the complex interplay between centralization and decentralization in media consumption, reflecting broader societal trends and the ongoing struggle to balance individual choice with accessibility and affordability.

This cycle between centralization and decentralization appears to be inevitable, repeating until an industry undergoes a fundamental transformation or becomes obsolete. It serves as a testament to the dynamic tension that shapes industries and consumer experiences alike.

Decentralized Finance: Redefining Money's Failure

Decentralized finance (DeFi) has emerged as an inspiration of hope for those seeking transparency and autonomy in financial dealings, challenging the long-standing dominance of centralized financial systems like those managed by the Federal Reserve and other central banks. For decades, these central banks have been the unchallenged conductors of our economic orchestras, controlling monetary policy to manage inflation and foster economic stability. However, their power to control the money supply, a key driver of inflation, can have widespread consequences.

Critics often highlight practices such as quantitative easing to illustrate how central banks can manipulate economies. By injecting money into the economy, they aim to stimulate growth, but this often results in inflated asset prices and diminished purchasing power for the average citizen. DeFi, operating on inherently decentralized blockchain technology, offers new possibilities in comparison to the centralized system. In DeFi, no single entity controls the entire framework. Instead, the power resides within a network of users participating in a transparent, open-source financial ecosystem. The core appeal of DeFi lies in its potential to provide an alternative to the traditional system, where decisions about money supply and inflation are made behind closed doors. DeFi operates without a central authority that prints money or makes unilateral economic decisions. These processes are instead governed by predetermined protocols, transparent to all, and immune to the influence of any single governing body.

DeFi extends the concept of decentralization beyond simple transactions, like those in Bitcoin, to encompass a broader range of financial services. Utilizing blockchain technology, often built on the Ethereum blockchain, DeFi platforms enable access to traditional financial services such as lending, borrowing, trading, insurance, and more, without the intermediation of traditional financial institutions.

Smart contracts are a crucial component of DeFi applications. These self-executing contracts have the terms of the agreement embedded directly in code, automating, and decentralizing financial services. While Bitcoin laid the groundwork for decentralized digital currencies, the DeFi movement represents a more expansive application of blockchain technology. It aims to decentralize a wide array of financial services, marking a significant step in the broader shift towards decentralization in finance. Both Bitcoin and DeFi play distinct yet complementary roles within this transformative movement.

Decentralization of Payments: Ending Unnecessary Middlemen

Traditionally, payment processors act as intermediaries in financial transactions, facilitating the transfer of money between parties. An example of a payment processing company is Mastercard Inc. However, with DeFi, the need for these types of intermediaries disappears. Blockchain technology enables direct peer-to-peer transactions, cutting out the middleman. This typically means faster transactions, lower fees, and a more streamlined process overall.

The landscape of payment processing is another area where the tension between centralization and decentralization becomes evident, particularly in how certain industries are treated. Current payment processors are often large, centralized entities that have been known to impose restrictive practices and standards on specific industries, regardless of the legality and legitimacy of the businesses within them.

Industries such as gambling, pornography, cannabis, and others often find themselves at a disadvantage. Despite operating legally and complying with regulations, these businesses frequently face higher interest rates and more stringent terms. They may also struggle with their ability to challenge fraudulent claims and access to a broad range of payment options. This situation is a clear reflection of the centralized control exerted by payment processors, which can arbitrarily decide the terms and conditions for businesses they deem as operating in 'high-risk' or 'undesirable' industries.

Moreover, the repercussions of these practices extend to consumers. Even if a business in one of these industries is approved by a payment processor, consumers may still face difficulties, such as being unable to use their credit or debit cards for transactions. This not only impacts the business's ability to operate smoothly but also restricts consumer choice and freedom.

This scenario underscores the need for more decentralized payment systems that can offer fairer, more equitable terms to all industries, particularly those unfairly marginalized by current systems. Decentralization in payment processing could lead to more inclusive financial practices, ensuring that legally compliant businesses, regardless of their industry, have equal access to payment services and are not subject to arbitrary or discrimina-tory practices. For consumers, this would mean greater freedom and flexibility in how they choose to spend their money, without the limitations imposed by centralized payment authorities.

The Fight for Decentralized Mail Delivery

Lysander Spooner, a 19th-century American entrepreneur and legal theorist, had a significant impact on the postal system, particularly in the realm of first-class mail. His story is a fascinat-ing example of challenging a government monopoly to promote decentralization and competition.

In the mid-1800s, the United States Postal Service (USPS) held a legal monopoly over the delivery of first-class mail. This meant that only the USPS could legally carry letters, and as a result, the costs for mailing letters were quite high. Spooner, a staunch advocate for free markets and individual liberty, saw this as an infringement on economic freedom and an opportu-nity to challenge the status quo.

In 1844, Spooner established the American Letter Mail Company, aiming to provide a cheaper and more efficient alter-native to the government-run postal service. He believed that competition would lead to better services and lower prices for consumers. Spooner's company charged lower rates for deliver-ing letters and quickly gained popularity among businesses and individuals who were frustrated with the high costs and ineffi-ciencies of the USPS.

One of Spooner's innovative strategies was the introduction of his own postage stamps. These stamps were used as a payment method for the services provided by the American Letter Mail Company. By designing and issuing his own stamps, Spooner was able to significantly undercut the prices of the USPS. His stamps were sold at lower rates than those of the government, making it more economical for individuals and businesses to send letters.

Spooner's venture directly challenged the government's monopoly on mail delivery. He argued that the federal government's control over mail was unconstitutional and that individuals had the right to choose how their mail was sent. His actions sparked a legal battle, as the government saw his business as an illegal enterprise.

Despite the legal challenges, Spooner's American Letter Mail Company succeeded in forcing the USPS to lower its rates and improve services. His efforts highlighted the benefits of competition and the drawbacks of a government monopoly. Ultimately, the government lowered its postal rates and improved its services, responding to the competition introduced by Spooner.

Spooner's impact on first-class mail is a classic example of how decentralization and competition can lead to better services and lower prices. His story demonstrates the power of individual initiative in challenging monopolies and promoting consumer choice. By taking on the postal monopoly, Spooner not only provided a valuable service to his contemporaries but also left a lasting legacy in the fight for economic freedom and the decentralization of services.

While Spooner's challenge against the centralized monopoly on first-class mail represented a fight for more competitive options via decentralization, the United States government responded by enacting restrictive laws. These laws stipulated that only the postmaster could deliver first-class mail to officially approved mailboxes, effectively barring anyone else from using these mailboxes. Additionally, the government declared that no other organizations were permitted to deliver first-class mail. These legislative measures effectively quashed any possibility of decentralizing or competing against the United States' monopoly on first-class mail delivery.

Proton Mail: Decentralization of Email Privacy

Proton Mail has significantly impacted the email service industry by championing privacy and decentralization. Before Proton Mail, most email services offered limited privacy features. Proton Mail introduced end-to-end encryption, ensuring that emails are encrypted from sender to receiver, making it difficult for third parties to intercept and read them. This was a major step towards decentralizing control over email privacy.

Unlike many other services that require personal information like phone numbers, Proton Mail allows users to create an email account without providing such details. This approach promotes a more decentralized and anonymous way of email communication, aligning with the ethos of privacy and user autonomy.

The open-source nature of Proton Mail is another significant aspect. It means anyone can review its code, ensuring there are no hidden backdoors or surveillance tools. Anyone can audit the code or pay for an independent security audit to ensure the code is secure. This transparency aligns with the decentralization principle, where trust is placed in the community rather than in a single entity.

Being based in Switzerland, a country known for strong privacy laws, Proton Mail offers additional data protection. This location choice means user data is protected by some of the most stringent privacy regulations globally, further decentralizing control from jurisdictions with looser privacy protections.

Proton Mail's success has also encouraged other email providers to adopt more secure and private practices, leading to a shift towards a more decentralized email ecosystem. Users now have more control over their data and privacy, a significant change from the traditional, more centralized email service models.

Furthermore, Proton Mail's commitment to privacy and security makes it a resistant force against censorship. This resistance is crucial for decentralization, as it prevents central authorities from having excessive control over information flow.

Essentially, Proton Mail has been a pioneer in promoting a more secure, private, and decentralized approach to email communication. Its emphasis on encryption, privacy, and user control has not only provided a valuable service to its users but also influenced the broader email service industry to prioritize privacy and decentralization.

Wrap up

Web3 is often thought of as synonymous with blockchain, but that's not the whole picture. It's like saying every dessert is a cake when, in reality, there's a whole world of sweets out there. Bitcoin and blockchain were the trailblazers, lighting the way for the broader concept of web3, which is really about shaking up the status quo through decentralization. This movement is like a breath of fresh air, bringing with it a host of benefits like owning your data, cutting out the middleman, and boosting security and transparency.

The common thread tying together the Zapatista movement, the evolution of cryptocurrencies, Netflix's disruption of traditional TV, the defiance of central banking norms, the efficiency of blockchain in financial transactions eliminating a need for payment processors, Lysander Spooner's postal service challenge, and Proton Mail's privacy-centric approach, is the power and potential of decentralization. Each example, in its own unique way, demonstrates how moving away from centralized control can lead to greater resilience, freedom of choice, transparency, efficiency, innovation, and privacy. These stories, from different domains and times, collectively illustrate a shift towards a future where decentralized systems empower individuals and communities, offering new models of operation and governance. This shift, emblematic of the Web3 movement, is a broader evolution in how we think about and organize our world, promising a realm where diversity, autonomy, and user empowerment are not just ideals, but realities.

| 4 |

Order and Strategy of Web3

Multiple Wallets

Before we discuss in more detail of the order and strategy in web3, it's important to understand that in the digital currency universe, a wallet is a virtual pocketbook where you keep your digital coins. Now, while most of us carry just one wallet in our day-to-day life, in the virtual world, having several is quite common, and there are good reasons for this.

Imagine splitting your money across different jars – one for savings, one for daily expenses, and another for a special treat. This is the idea behind multiple digital wallets. It's about organizing and compartmentalizing. For safety's sake, you wouldn't want to keep all your savings in an easily accessible jar on your windowsill. This is where the concept of 'cold' and 'hot' wallets comes into play. A cold wallet is like a secure vault buried deep underground, holding your most treasured possessions. Its private key is not stored on a computer or online, so it's less vulnerable. On the other hand, a hot wallet is more like a money jar on your kitchen table – always within reach, but also more exposed. To use the value stored safely underground without always accessing it, you could keep a representative note in your money jar. In digital terms, this means the main assets stay protected in the cold wallet, but their value, or voting power, can still be utilized via the hot wallet.

Having multiple wallets provides another layer of safety. If one wallet gets hacked or compromised, not all is lost. And with assets safely stored, individuals might feel more inclined to be active participants in the digital community, using and trading their coins or casting votes on community matters.

However, every coin has two sides. Having numerous wallets might allow a single person to exert more influence in community decisions. This is like one individual having many voices. This is because a wallet is pseudo-anonymous where the string of what looks like a random set of letters and numbers (also called a hash) are what identifies your wallet. The public can always see the Public Address (those "random set of letters and numbers") of our wallet, but do NOT have a way to identify who owns it or has possession of it. This means that it can be used to distort the perception of consensus and fairness. And if it becomes known that a few individuals have disproportionate sway because of their many wallets, it can stir distrust within the community.

While having more than one digital wallet can be favored to having various pockets for different needs, it's imperative to use them responsibly and maintain the collective trust and balance of the digital community. Multiple Wallets can also open the door to multiple identities – keep this in mind for later. With the understanding of the ability to have multiple wallets, you will find there are many ways they can be used in the web3 space.

Organizational Structures

As we discussed earlier in the book, in a centralized corporate structure, the flow of information is primarily upward. Operational insights, market data, and performance metrics move from the specialized departments to the executive management, and finally, to the board of directors. This hierarchy is designed for efficiency and effective decision-making but also creates certain challenges and limitations.

One of the primary challenges lies in the potential disconnect between the board of directors and the broader stakeholders, which may include not only shareholders but also employees, customers, and even the general public. While board members are ostensibly elected to represent shareholder interests, they often operate in a somewhat insulated environment, commonly referred to as the "boardroom bubble."

Within this "bubble," board members may receive filtered or curated information, which can create a gap between their perception and the actual sentiments or needs of the broader stakeholder community. For example, while a proposed strategic shift might look promising in a board presentation, employees at the operational level might have firsthand insights suggesting otherwise. Similarly, shareholders might have diverse opinions that aren't fully represented by the board, and customers' needs may evolve faster than the board's strategies can adapt.

Furthermore, the board's decisions and strategic directions are typically long-term, meaning they might not always reflect immediate concerns or short-term desires of stakeholders. As a result, the board may make decisions that seem disconnected or even contrary to public sentiment or immediate stakeholder needs.

The hierarchical, centralized nature of corporate structures thus has a double-edged sword quality. While it allows for efficient decision-making and clear lines of authority, it also poses a risk of isolating the board of directors from the nuanced and dynamic realities of their stakeholders, which could ultimately impact the organization's adaptability and long-term success.

Decentralized Autonomous Organizations (DAOs) represent a groundbreaking shift from traditional, centralized governance models. At their core, DAOs operate on digital platforms governed by smart contracts, often built on blockchain technology. This transparent and immutable setup brings a radical change to how governance and decision-making unfold. Rather than centralizing power in a board of directors or executive team, DAOs rely on smart contracts to create a governance framework that's automatically enforced by a decentralized network of nodes. This design ensures rule adherence without requiring a centralized authority.

In simple terms, think of a DAO like a direct democracy, except the number of votes is based on the amount of interest you have in the organization. Let's say there are 100 tokens total. In this case, think of tokens being like shares of a company. If you own 5 tokens of the 100 tokens, your votes on proposals will have 5% of an impact on the outcome if everyone votes.

Most DAOs also will allow all members to be able to make proposals. However, others may require a certain number of tokens to create a proposal. Once you are part of a DAO, you will have a say. There's no C-suite that leads the organization's direction, all progress is made by its members.

Tokens or cryptocurrencies serve as the lifeblood of this model, incentivizing community participation in a way like shares in a traditional company. These digital assets typically offer voting rights and, often, a share in the organization's success, further democratizing governance. Interactions within the DAO typically happen via specialized user interfaces that encourage democratic engagement. These platforms enable individual members not only to interact but also to influence the DAO's operations and future direction, empowering a member-driven approach to governance.

The transition from centralization to decentralization has its obstacles, particularly when it comes to ethical considerations. The democratization of governance disperses decision-making power among many stakeholders, making ethical frameworks vitally important. This is where a "voting code of ethics" comes into play. It acts as a guiding framework for responsible, transparent, and fair community action.

A central tenet of any such code is the need to maintain the integrity and fairness of the voting process. This is achieved through safeguards against fraud, corruption, and other misconduct that could compromise electoral legitimacy. The goal would be to use blockchain as a way to validate the integrity of each vote.

Another critical ethical principle revolves around respecting the rights of all eligible voters. Beyond merely offering the ability to vote, this also entails protecting voter privacy and freedom from coercion or intimidation. In a democratic space as open as a DAO, it's crucial to establish conditions that allow the democratic process to flourish unhindered.

Transparency allows demanding clear instructions for voters and accessible information about candidates or proposals. By keeping all relevant details in the public eye, including voting records and outcomes, DAOs can fortify community trust and engagement. Moreover, data protection is imperative; even within the transparent nature of blockchain transactions, stringent measures must be in place to encrypt voter registration databases and control access to this sensitive information.

The security of the voting process itself is vital. This involves sophisticated strategies to counter potential cyber threats and other interferences that could compromise the integrity of the vote. Utilizing decentralized networks for real-time monitoring against suspicious activities adds an additional layer of security, mitigating the risks associated with centralized points of failure.

Keep in mind that in a DAO, voters are actively participating as they exercise a power like that of politicians in traditional governance systems. Having this decision-making power comes accountability. Stakeholders are directly responsible for their choices, much like how politicians are held accountable in representative democracies.

When determining the ethical dimensions of decentralized governance, we recognize that DAOs must adhere to robust ethical guidelines to ensure integrity, fairness, and trust. Yet, these principles are also contingent on the voting systems DAOs deploy. These systems define how its stakeholders make collective decisions. Within the realm of voting, key systems like anonymous voting, public voting, and game theory voting come into focus.

Anonymous Voting

The concept of anonymous voting in a Decentralized Autonomous Organization (DAO) has its advantages and disadvantages. Anonymous voting in a DAO is like having an invisibility cloak. It offers a layer of privacy that allows members to cast their votes without revealing their identities. This feature empowers members to express their true opinions without fear of backlash, fostering a democratic spirit within the organization. However, if voting is the only anonymous aspect while the community members are known to each other, it can lead to manipulation, collusion, and backdoor deals. Even though a group may know how they voted, the broader community would be unable to pinpoint who colluded in favor of proposals that may be disadvantageous to the majority.

The lack of accountability in anonymous voting is analogous to a masquerade ball, where it's difficult to discern who's behind each mask. This can be problematic, especially if decisions lead to negative outcomes. Ensuring the integrity of the voting process in a DAO, where trust is paramount, becomes significantly more challenging when votes are cast anonymously. It's essential to have a robust system to prevent vote rigging and ensure fairness, but this is complicated when voters are hidden behind the veil of anonymity.

Moreover, anonymous voting can sometimes erode trust within the community. If members feel that the voting process lacks transparency, it can lead to doubts and suspicions, potentially undermining the cohesion and stability of the DAO.

Anonymous voting in a DAO is a complex issue that requires careful consideration. It offers the benefits of privacy and fairness but also brings challenges in terms of accountability and maintaining trust. Navigating this decision involves weighing the advantages of privacy against the potential risks to the organization's integrity and unity.

Public Voting

Public or transparent voting in a DAO is where every choice is public for all to see. This shift from the shadows of anonymity to the glare of transparency can be a jarring experience, especially for those accustomed to the veil of privacy in traditional voting systems.

Imagine every vote you cast is an open book, a scenario that's routine in political systems like the United States Congress. When Congress votes on a bill, their decisions are recorded publicly. In such a system, every decision, every lean towards a choice is out there for scrutiny, discussion, and sometimes, even debate. This level of openness is a new playing field for many in the Web3 community, particularly those who have explored anonymous voting systems.

In the realm of DAOs, this transparency brings with it a heavy cloak of accountability. It's like standing in a glass house where every move you make is visible to your neighbors. This can be a daunting prospect, especially considering the multifaceted identities one can hold in the Web3 world. The challenge here is not just about being open with your choices but also about standing by them, ready to field questions and sometimes defend your stance. It's a far cry from the anonymous ballot where your vote is your secret.

Critics from the Web2 era often argue that DAO members are not politicians and shouldn't be subjected to the same level of scrutiny. However, in a landscape where trust and confidence are as valuable as currency, transparency becomes a crucial element. Without it, building trust and confidence in the system can be an uphill battle.

With public or transparent voting in a DAO, it's about owning that vote in the full light of day. It's a commitment to transparency that goes beyond the act of voting, extending into the realm of accountability and trust. This approach may challenge the norms of privacy and anonymity that many in the Web3 space hold dear, but it also opens the door to a more accountable, trustworthy, and ultimately resilient community.

On the bright side, transparent voting is where everyone can see the votes being casted. This visibility acts as a strong deterrent against fraudulent voting. It's like having a community watch program where everyone keeps an eye out, ensuring fair play. This level of openness also encourages voters to think more carefully about their choices, knowing that their decisions are out in the open for all to see. Additionally, the ability to audit votes on the blockchain adds another layer of security and integrity to the process, much like having a tamper-proof seal on the ballot box. With Blockchain, you don't have to worry about miscounts.

However, transparency can have some drawbacks. The visibility of each vote can be like a spotlight that some might find too bright. It can lead to coercion and intimidation, as voters might feel pressured to vote in a certain way, fearing backlash if they go against the majority or powerful individuals in the DAO. This environment of peer pressure can influence voters to make choices that don't align with their true preferences, skewing the election results. Moreover, the fear of public scrutiny might discourage some members from participating at all, especially those who value their privacy or are wary of potential consequences. This can affect the representative nature of the election, turning it into a parade where only the boldest march. Knowing how your friends voted, may also sway your decision when voting, ultimately leading to "groupthink."

Public voting in a DAO is a balancing act between fostering accountability and maintaining individual freedom. It's about finding the sweet spot where transparency doesn't become a tool for manipulation but serves as a foundation for a fair and democratic decision-making process. The challenge lies in creating an environment where members feel safe to express their true opinions, ensuring that the DAO remains a vibrant and representative community.

The Pseudonymous Structure in Cryptocurrency Voting Systems

In a pseudonymous setting like the Ethereum network, where users can possess multiple wallets (as we mentioned earlier), the lines between accountability and freedom blur. On the one side, pseudonymity can offer a shield against coercion or societal pressure, similar to anonymous voting. It allows participants to cast votes without immediate identification, which can be liberating and lead to more genuine input. This also can make it so the voting can be public, without identifying the wallet holder. Everyone will know the wallet and how they voted, but no one will know who owns the wallet, unless they choose to reveal themselves or get doxed (identity getting revealed involuntarily by another person).

Alternately, pseudonymity can often embolden individuals to act with less accountability. When people feel detached from the repercussions of their decisions, there's a tendency to prioritize self-interest, even at the community's expense. This is especially problematic when one considers the potential for "Sybil attacks," where a single entity controls multiple nodes or accounts to unduly influence network decisions.

Game Theory and Voting

In DAOs, stakeholders must choose between personal gain and the community's well-being. The Nash equilibrium, a cornerstone concept in game theory, serves as a guiding principle in these complex dynamics. The Nash Equilibrium declares that in a game or situation where more than 2 players cannot cooperate, each player makes the best strategic decision they can for themselves, assuming others are doing the same. Ideally, this equilibrium encourages each voter to act in the collective interest of the community. However, Nash equilibrium is not the ideal, it's the most common response when both players act selfishly without knowing what the other players would do. It's the optimal decision for the individual player, which is not the optimal decision for the group.

The dynamics of voting in a DAO can draw parallels to the classic Prisoner's Dilemma, a scenario that vividly illustrates the complexities of trust and decision-making in a decentralized environment.

In the Prisoner's Dilemma, two suspects are placed in a situation where they must choose between cooperating with each other or acting selfishly, without knowing what the other will do. While in separate interrogation rooms, the prisoners must choose between two choices: to "rat/snitch" (share evidence) on the other prisoner or remain silent to the detective. The optimal outcome for both is achieved through cooperation which is to remain silent, but the uncertainty and lack of communication (due to being in another room) often lead to both choosing the selfish option which is to "rat" on the other. This results in a less favorable outcome for both, known as the Nash Equilibrium, where each player's strategy is optimal given the other's strategy.

Translating this to the context of a DAO, the dilemma manifests in the voting process. In a decentralized system, especially one with transparent voting, members can see each other's choices, but this visibility doesn't necessarily enable them to influence or change these decisions. This scenario becomes even more complex when considering members with significant voting power. If these influential members choose to act selfishly, prioritizing their interests, and the majority acts altruistically, the outcome can disproportionately benefit the few at the expense of the many.

However, if everyone in the DAO opts for the selfish route, the outcome might not be the worst possible, but it certainly won't be the best either. It's a delicate balance where the collective good hinges on the individual choices of its members. The decentralized nature of the DAO means that these decisions are made independently, without a central authority to guide or influence them. This independence is both the strength and the challenge of decentralized systems.

Real-world conditions often diverge from idealized theories. In this case, the temptation to vote selfishly for short-term gains will lead to less optimal community outcomes. This form of behavior can not only weaken trust within a DAO but can also contribute to reduced voter participation over time. It's an internal governance failure comparable to the "Tragedy of the Commons," where individual selfish actions lead to collective detriment.

The Italian Mafia in the United States, often known for their secretive and organized nature, were quite effective in manipulating situations to their advantage. They achieved this through a combination of their centralized power structure and a strict code known as Omertà. This code emphasized silence, honor, and specific conduct among its members.

Omertà played a crucial role in the Mafia's operations. It essentially meant that members were sworn to secrecy and were not allowed to talk about the organization's activities to outsiders. This vow of silence ensured that internal matters stayed within the group, making it difficult for law enforcement to penetrate or gather evidence against them.

This code was used to disrupt the Nash Equilibrium. Instead of making a selfish response due to not knowing what the other party would do, this code would give them and their friends the ability to uphold that code to remain silent and give a more favorable outcome to all the involved parties. If they had witnesses to a crime they committed and those witnesses were not members who followed their code, they would use violence to persuade the witnesses to remain silent or be unhelpful to the authorities.

The Mafia's centralized power meant that decisions and orders came from the top and were followed without question by those lower in the hierarchy. This structure allowed them to coordinate their activities effectively and maintain a tight grip on their operations. While this style of collusion is not condoned by many, it was effective and worth mentioning. Collusion like this has occurred in web3, but instead of violence being a deterrent for snitching, bribery to remain silent seems to be more common.

The Prisoner's Dilemma within a DAO context underscores the importance of trust and cooperation in decentralized systems. It highlights the need for mechanisms that encourage collaborative decision-making and align individual incentives with the collective good. Besides transparency and visibility of actions, it is important to uphold a shared commitment to the overarching goals and values of the DAO. It's a complex dance of individual choices and collective outcomes, where the harmony of the group depends on the steps of its individual members.

The Accountability Dilemma

Here, we reencounter the core dilemmas of game theory and the Nash equilibrium. While pseudonymous actors may think their singular decisions don't affect the system at large, or that others will make altruistic choices to balance things out, this mindset can lead to suboptimal outcomes for the entire community. Pseudonymity, then, poses a unique challenge to achieving a Nash equilibrium, as it dilutes the direct feeling of responsibility that comes from identifiable participation.

The balance of community decisions in a DAO is a delicate ecosystem, much like a coral reef where each organism plays a vital role in maintaining the health of the whole. When decisions in a DAO become skewed towards selfish interests, it can disrupt this balance, potentially leading to the devaluation of the entire community.

In a DAO, fairness and equity in decision-making are not just idealistic goals, they are essential for the survival and prosperity of the organization. If the voting system becomes biased, favoring certain parties over others, it can erode the collective trust and interest that are the basis of the community. Think of this situation as if the crew of a ship only looks out for themselves, ignoring the wellbeing of the vessel. Eventually, this selfishness can lead to the ship sinking, taking everyone down with it, including those who acted selfishly.

The value of a DAO lies in its collective spirit and the shared vision of its members. When the decision-making process becomes unfairly tilted towards certain individuals or groups, it undermines the very principles of decentralization and collective governance that define a DAO. This can lead to a loss of interest and participation from the broader community, diminishing the DAO's value and effectiveness.

Therefore, it's imperative for a DAO to maintain a fair and balanced decision-making process. This involves ensuring that the voting system is transparent, equitable, and reflects the interests of the entire community. By doing so, a DAO can preserve its integrity, retain its value, and continue to thrive as a collaborative and democratic entity.

Voting Power

In a Decentralized Autonomous Organization (DAO), the dynamics of decision-making are inherently tied to the concept of voting power (VP). So how does one acquire this Voting Power? The process often starts with the tokens or cryptocurrency a member holds. It's worth mentioning that this framework isn't exclusive to fungible tokens; even non-fungible tokens (NFTs) can serve as the backbone of a DAO in a specific community.

Acquiring voting power can be as straightforward as purchasing tokens, either from the DAO itself or from existing members in a secondary exchange (an open marketplace). This approach is the most straightforward, but it's not the only path to influence. For instance, some DAOs implement reward systems to incentivize contributions to the community. Let's say you submit a software fix or suggest a new project initiative. In return for that contribution, you might receive tokens that augment your voting power.

Another intriguing avenue for bolstering your influence within a DAO involves staking tokens. This concept will be familiar to anyone who has participated in proof-of-stake (PoS) blockchain networks. By staking, or locking up your tokens, you commit to the network for a set period and can receive increased voting power as a reward for your loyalty. It's important to recognize that the avenues for acquiring voting power are not set in stone as all DAO's have unique rules and governance structures.

Obtaining voting power in a DAO is a multifaceted endeavor that is influenced by factors such as token ownership, contributions, staking, etc. While this power structure enables a decentralized model of governance, it also paves the way for 'whales' to exert significant influence. Yet, the impact of such influence is moderated by the specific governance protocols of the DAO in question. Therefore, both new members and whales alike must follow and interact with the DAO's rules and incentives to participate meaningfully in its collective decision-making process.

Conflict of Interest

It's very common to see the concept of "conflict of interest" as a standard that guides professionals to act with transparency and avoid personal biases. These age-old principles, emphasizing fairness and integrity, find their strongest expression in professions such as law and medicine. Here, rules are rigorously enforced to uphold public trust, ensuring professionals prioritize their clients or patients over any personal gain.

In the web3 space, the guidelines that have served as ethical compasses in the traditional world become harder to enforce. The absence of centralized authorities, combined with the potential veil of anonymity or ability to make multiple identities by simply creating new wallets and social media profiles, makes this terrain complex and unprecedented.

The very pillars of web3 – the promises of decentralization, community governance, and anonymity – also pose as its most intricate mazes. While web3 brings freedom, it also brings responsibility to the individual. The absence of established checks and balances by a centralized entity brings out the need for elevated awareness, identifying patterns amongst multiple identities and more. The multi-role dynamics gets intense because an individual might juggle roles across projects, weave a web of overlapping interests that's challenging to decode.

The web3 advocates, guided by the foundational principles of blockchain are collectively pushing towards ethical clarity. With discussions around on-chain governance and transparent decision-making gathering momentum, the community is striving to build trust and ensure accountability. The path to navigating conflicts of interest in this revolutionary domain is dotted with challenges, but as with any frontier, it's an evolving narrative, fueled by learning and adaptation.

Whales

In the world of DAOs, a "whale" refers to someone who owns a large amount of the organization's tokens, and therefore, holds significant voting power. Now, let's imagine this in a real-world context. Think of a small-town meeting where everyone gets to vote on community issues. In a balanced setting, everyone's vote would have equal weight, ensuring a fair decision-making process. But what if one person owns most of the land in town? That person's voice might drown out everyone else's, making it hard for the community to make decisions that benefit everyone.

Being a "whale" in a Decentralized Autonomous Organization (DAO) isn't all sunshine and rainbows. Sure, you have a lot of voting power, but with great power comes great responsibility—and scrutiny.

Imagine being the star player on a sports team. While you might be the one making the most goals, you also bear the weight of expectation. If you miss an important shot, you don't just let yourself down, you also let the whole team down. The same can be true for whales in a DAO. One wrong decision, and they risk alienating the community, potentially causing members to lose faith and abandon the DAO altogether. In the worst-case scenario, a mass exodus could devalue the tokens, leading to a collapse of the organization.

When multiple whales are active in a DAO, their combined voting power can be so overwhelming that it drowns out the voices of smaller token holders. It's like being in a classroom where two or three students are so vocal that others start thinking, "Why bother raising my hand? The teacher is only listening to them anyway." This dynamic can create a sense of helplessness among community members, making them feel as though their contributions are worthless.

Interestingly, being a responsible whale isn't just a matter of not abusing power, it's also about the complexities of when and how to use that power for the greater good. If a whale genuinely cares about the community's well-being, voting on proposals can be a real dilemma. Each choice has consequences for the club's future and its members. Similarly, the whale must weigh each decision carefully, as it affects not only their holdings but the entire DAO's trajectory.

And what if they decide to sell some of their tokens to reduce their influence? That comes with its own set of challenges. Dumping a large number of tokens on the market could destabilize the token's value, inadvertently harming the community they wish to protect. It can also cause others in that organization to sell out of fear.

So yes, being a whale in a DAO might offer power and influence, but it's a role fraught with its own set of challenges, decisions, and responsibilities. It's a balancing act that requires a keen understanding of community dynamics and collective well-being.

In DAOs, which are meant to be decentralized and democratic, the presence of a whale can somewhat paradoxically steer the organization toward centralization. How? Well, because the whale has so much voting power, their decisions can overwhelmingly influence the course of the DAO, sometimes to the detriment of other members. This can lead to a kind of unofficial centralization of power within a system that's supposed to be all about distributing power equally.

But that's not the only concern. With enough voting power, a whale could potentially take actions that benefit them personally, even if those actions are not in the best interests of the community. For example, they could vote to allocate the DAO's funds in a way that disproportionately benefits them, or even drain the DAO's financial reserves, leaving little for other initiatives or members.

While DAOs aim for a balanced and fair system, the presence of whales introduces the risk of centralization and self-interested behavior. Imagine being a kid on a playground where all the kids are supposed to share the toys, but one kid brings in a huge toy box and insists on making the rules. Sure, they're part of the community, but their outsized influence can tip the scales and disrupt the harmony.

This highlights the importance of designing DAOs and other decentralized systems with safeguards against the undue influence of whales, thereby ensuring that the spirit of decentralization remains intact.

White hats and Vigilantes

Picture a close-knit community that has its own well, a primary source of water that everyone relies on. One day, someone starts poisoning the well. The community is unaware that the poisoner is actually one of their own, working quietly to jeopardize their well-being. Now, imagine a "vigilante," a well-intentioned member who discovers what's happening and tries to alert the community. Ironically, this vigilante faces skepticism and suspicion because no one else has noticed the poisoner's activities yet.

The vigilante is in a tight spot. On one hand, they have vital information that could save the community; on the other, they risk becoming an outcast, viewed as someone trying to sow discord. This is a critical moment. The vigilante starts by approaching individuals they trust, convincing them one by one of the impending danger. Slowly, a group of like-minded individuals forms to confront the poisoner, taking on the role of "white hat vigilantes."

However, they must tread carefully. If they're too aggressive, they risk alienating the very community they're trying to save. But doing nothing isn't an option either, as the poisoner continues to act against the community's interests. As they gain more support and the evidence becomes more compelling, the balance starts to tip. The community begins to realize who the real enemy is, uniting to confront and remove the threat.

This situation, while dramatic, mirrors what can happen within a DAO where bad actors, whether they are rogue whales or a coalition of voters, can act against the community's interest. DAOs are particularly vulnerable to such activities because of their decentralized nature, which makes it harder to enforce rules or vet members effectively.

The existence of vigilantes or "white hats" is essential for the health of these decentralized communities. But their success often hinges on the community's willingness to listen, to question the status quo, and to act when action is necessary. When vigilantes win these battles, it can set a precedent, making it harder for bad actors to exploit the system in the future. But vigilance must be ongoing. The battle between community defenders and would-be exploiters is never definitively won.

Next time you join a decentralized community, keep your eyes open. The vigilantes among you might be your best line of defense against those who would poison the well. And who knows, you might even find yourself taking up the white hat to protect something you believe in.

Rug Pulls

A "rug pull" in the world of Web3 gets its meaning from the concept "to pull the rug out from under someone," which means to suddenly withdraw support or pull off an unexpected trick. It's like recalling those magic shows where a magician swiftly pulls a tablecloth from under a set of dishes without disturbing them. However, in a rug pull, it's as if the magician yanks the cloth slowly, causing everything to crash down. In this scenario, developers or insiders of a project entice investors with attractive promises. But instead of delivering on these promises, they abruptly disappear, taking the investors' money with them. It's a deceptive maneuver where the magic trick fails, leaving investors in a lurch.

One common setting for a rug pull is a scenario filled with hype and promises of high returns. Projects that sound too good to be true often are. They hook unsuspecting investors and, once a substantial sum is collected, the creators disappear into the digital ether. This deceit is further facilitated when the developers or founders behind these projects remain anonymous.

Without a face or real-world identity tied to a project, it's far easier to execute a scam and escape the consequences.

Code plays a crucial role in many rug pulls. Projects that have skipped third-party code audits or reviews might harbor hidden malicious intents. There could be concealed functions in the token's code, allowing creators to craft new tokens from thin air, which dilutes the token's value. These freshly minted tokens can then be sold all together, wreaking havoc on the project's economy.

Another technical maneuver is through liquidity tactics in DeFi projects. Liquidity can be a beacon of trust, but it can also be quickly yanked away. In a typical rug pull, there's a sudden drain of all liquidity from a pool. This move leaves investors stranded, unable to trade or claim their money. Furthermore, the dangers aren't limited to the tokens or liquidity pools. Entire fake decentralized exchanges (DEX) have been created, perfectly mimicking genuine platforms, designed to trap and defraud unsuspecting users.

Pre-sales have also been arenas for mischief. Developers might roll out a pre-sale of tokens, drawing significant investments. However, instead of using these funds for the promised project development, they disappear as soon as the pre-sale ends. In some cases, to appear genuine, projects lock up tokens for a set period, claiming it's to stabilize the token price. But this might merely be a ruse to gain trust and draw more money before the rug is pulled.

Lastly, though not a traditional rug pull, "pump and dumps" bear mentioning. Influencers or large token holders might drive up a token's price, only to sell off their stash suddenly, leaving their followers or smaller investors holding the worthless bags.

Navigating the cryptocurrency world requires caution. It's imperative to research thoroughly, seek projects with audited codes, understand token mechanisms, and be wary of projects shrouded in too much mystery.

Ramping up effect

The "ramping up" effect in the context of cryptocurrency and media refers to the increasing intensity and frequency of promotional efforts aimed at generating heightened interest and excitement around a specific coin or project. This phenomenon originates in traditional finance and stock promotion. In those contexts, some might recognize it as part of the "pump and dump" strategies, where there's a lot of hype created around a particular asset to artificially inflate its price before those in the know sell off for a profit.

When it comes to strategies used to ramp up interest in the crypto world, these often involve a surge in content creation by "shillers" and media outlets. This can manifest as an influx of articles, blog posts, or YouTube videos discussing the merits of the coin or project. Additionally, there's usually a noticeable buzz on social media. Influencers, enthusiasts, and sometimes even bots might begin posting more about the specific crypto-currency, using trending hashtags or creating memes to help it go viral. Engagement in crypto-focused communities, such as those on Reddit, Telegram, or Discord, also tends to increase. Often, projects might strategically time their announcements of partnerships, integrations, or endorsements to feed into this growing hype.

The outcomes of this ramping up can vary. On the one hand, if the increased attention is a result of genuine interest and valid developments, it could lead to wider adoption of the coin and perhaps a rise in its valuation. However, if the increased attention is driven by speculative or manipulative intent without substantial developments to back up the hype, it can lead to significant volatility. Late investors especially might suffer financial losses, and the reputation of the project could be damaged.

It's vital for investors to differentiate between a genuine increase in interest and an artificially created buzz. Approaching investment decisions with a healthy dose of skepticism, conducting thorough research, and seeking information from a variety of reputable sources can help in making informed decisions. Ethical considerations are also crucial, as deceptive ramping up can lead to unsuspecting investors getting burned. It's always a good idea to approach any investment, especially in the volatile world of crypto, with caution.

| 5 |

The Web3 Revolution

Many of us use the internet daily for our apps on our phone or to interact and engage with others on social media. Right now, being part of the web2 ideology, not many people are used to digital ownership. The web3 revolution is an exciting new era of the internet that's about to change everything we know about digital interaction, ownership, and value creation.

Founded on the principles of decentralization, user empowerment, and transparent technology, web3 is a complete reimagination of our existing internet. It's an exciting shift from the centralized, corporation-dominated web2 to a place where the common person will have a real stake in the digital spaces we inhabit.

At the center of this revolution is the concept of Tokenization. It's about turning tangible and intangible assets into digital tokens, making them easily tradable and accessible on the blockchain. This is a complete cultural shift, redefining how we perceive value and ownership in the digital age.

This leads us to NFTs, or Non-Fungible Tokens. These unique digital assets are transforming everything from art and music to gaming and content creation. NFTs establish a new form of digital property rights, where creators can monetize their work in ways never before possible.

You can even tokenize Attention as a currency. In a world where our attention is bombarded by endless streams of content, web3 recognizes its value. Platforms like the Brave Browser and the Basic Attention Token (BAT) are pioneering ways to reward users for their engagement, turning attention into a tangible asset.

Metaverses take these tokens and implement them to make a lot of these digital concepts real. Imagine virtual worlds where you can live, work, play, and interact in environments limited only by imagination. These digital realms offer unprecedented opportunities for self-expression, cultural exploration, and new forms of social interaction, blurring the lines between the physical and digital worlds.

The web3 revolution is a paradigm shift in how we interact with the digital world. It's about giving power back to the users, creating new forms of value, and opening a universe of possibilities that redefine the boundaries of creativity, commerce, and connection.

Cryptocurrencies

The web3 revolution began with Bitcoin. Created in 2009 by an individual or group of people using the pseudonym Satoshi Nakamoto, Bitcoin introduced a new kind of "money." It was digital, decentralized, and based on blockchain technology. This was the first currency that was not controlled by a government entity. It was secure, independent, and enabled direct transactions from person to person with the middlemen being the miners that are decentralized all around the world.

Bitcoin's innovation lay in its decentralized nature, where no single entity controlled the currency. Its public ledger brought unprecedented transparency to all transactions. Utilizing blockchain technology, Bitcoin effectively prevented double spending. This technology also made it extremely challenging for hackers to increase the Bitcoin supply on the blockchain. The only feasible way to do this would be to control over 50% of the network's miners, either by hacking a majority of them or by deploying a vast number of their own miners.

The strength of blockchain lies in the decentralization of its network, which safeguards it against malicious attacks. This technology significantly reduces costs for several reasons. It's accessible to anyone, including businesses, eliminating the need for expensive internal or outsourced server solutions. Traditional server setups come with high costs: pricey hardware, dedicated space, specialized cooling systems, and ongoing maintenance. Outsourcing servers also means entrusting a third party with data security and relying on their maintenance.

Blockchain addresses these issues effectively. Since it's run by miners globally, it doesn't have a single point of vulnerability to hacking. The chances of network downtime are almost nil, and the costs associated with using the network are shared among all users. This means businesses can access superior technology and a more reliable network at a fraction of the cost of traditional methods, with enhanced security.

Cryptocurrencies extend far beyond the realm of digital currency, challenging the conventional views held by many in the web2 space. Their applications are varied and multifaceted. Beyond facilitating secure and anonymous transactions, which cater to privacy concerns, cryptocurrencies play a significant role in asset tokenization. This involves digitizing real-world assets like real estate, streamlining the transaction process.

Moreover, many cryptocurrencies function as Software As A Service (SAAS) applications. They offer practical solutions for brands, such as combating product counterfeiting, enhancing shipping logistics, and outsourcing CPU tasks. They're also instrumental in areas like copyrighting and more.

The list of utilities cryptocurrencies provide is extensive and continually growing, with many yet to be discovered or fully realized. The web3 revolution, ignited by Bitcoin and propelled forward by Ethereum's introduction of smart contracts, continues to expand. An increasing number of cryptocurrencies are being developed to address a wide array of challenges. This technology is poised to be widely adopted and integrated into various sectors, marking a significant shift in how we interact with and leverage digital solutions.

Tokenization

Tokenization is a huge part of the web3 revolution. It represents a transformative approach to digital assets and currency. This concept allows for virtually any item, whether tangible or intangible, to be converted into a digital token. This process significantly decentralizes the concept of currency, eliminating the need for intermediaries in transactions and trading.

To understand tokenization, consider the evolution of trade and currency. Historically, trade began with bartering, where goods were directly exchanged. For example, a chicken farmer might trade poultry for corn or blacksmith services. However, this system was flawed due to the varying intrinsic values of different goods. To address this, banks introduced banknotes tied to a stable asset like gold, creating a standardized medium for equitable trade. This system evolved into our current government-backed currency model. However, this model is not without its flaws, as seen when currencies become unpegged from their gold standard, leading to potential inflation and decreased purchasing power.

Tokenization offers an alternative to government-issued currency. It enables specific assets, like 1 banana being able to be traded for a fraction of a chicken, to be represented as tokens with set values. This democratizes currency, allowing individuals to trade in units of their choosing. Moreover, tokenization extends beyond mere currency. It involves creating digital versions of various assets such as art, real estate, or music, on the blockchain. These digital versions, or tokens, act as certificates of ownership or fractions of the asset itself.

The advantages of tokenization are manifold. It simplifies and accelerates the process of buying, selling, and trading assets. For instance, one can easily invest in a fraction of a renowned painting or a property abroad through digital platforms. This breaks down traditional barriers in asset management, offering greater accessibility and inclusivity. Investments in high-value assets like art or real estate, typically reserved for the affluent, become accessible to a broader audience through fractional ownership.

Tokenization also introduces unprecedented levels of security and transparency. The blockchain's immutable nature ensures a reliable and tamper-proof record of ownership, mitigating concerns about fraud or counterfeit assets. Furthermore, it streamlines asset management by reducing paperwork, cutting out middlemen, and enhancing transaction speed and cost-effectiveness.

Beyond physical assets, tokenization can apply to personal data, content creation, and online activities. It opens up possibilities for individuals to earn tokens for their digital contributions, such as writing reviews or creating content. Tokens can even represent time or services, offering a new dimension to how we perceive and trade value.

Tokenizing Your Attention

The integration of the Brave Browser and the Basic Attention Token (BAT) exemplifies a novel approach to tokenization in the digital realm, particularly within the context of the web3 revolution. This innovative concept reimagines the traditional web browsing experience, placing a significant emphasis on the value of user engagement and attention in the digital economy.

The Brave Browser separates itself from conventional web browsers by recognizing and monetizing user attention. In an era where individuals spend considerable time online, engaging with content and advertisements, Brave posits a groundbreaking idea: user attention is not just valuable, it's a commodity that can be tokenized.

The Basic Attention Token, or BAT, stands as a unique cryptocurrency designed for this very purpose. It goes beyond the standard functions of digital currencies, focusing instead on rewarding users for their engagement with digital content. As users interact with ads on Brave, they accumulate BAT, effectively turning their attention and time into tangible digital assets.

This approach is deeply intertwined with the principles of web3, which advocates for a decentralized, user-centric internet. Brave and BAT disrupt the traditional digital advertising model, which predominantly benefits large corporations, and reallocate value back to the users – the true viewers of these ads. This redistribution of value is a quintessential example of tokenization, where user engagement is quantified and rewarded in a tangible form.

Tokenizing attention in this manner is a transformative development in the digital advertising space. It empowers users, transforming them from passive recipients of ads to active stakeholders in the advertising ecosystem. This model not only recognizes the value of user attention but also compensates them for it, embodying the ethos of a tokenized economy.

Moreover, Brave Browser's commitment to privacy and efficiency complements its tokenization strategy. By blocking trackers and unwanted ads, Brave ensures a faster, more secure browsing experience. This not only rewards users in the form of tokens but also enhances the overall quality of their online interactions.

The Brave Browser and BAT are at the forefront of a new wave of tokenization, offering a glimpse into the future of the internet – a future where user attention is not only recognized as valuable but is also tokenized and rewarded. This innovative approach aligns with the web3 vision, paving the way for a more equitable, user-empowered digital landscape.

* * *

The concept of tokenization as a whole, is a critical element in the web3 space, redefining asset accessibility, transaction security, and efficiency. It heralds a new era of digital ownership and value, democratizing asset access and creating innovative avenues for earning and owning in the digital age. This shift in how we view ownership and value is a thrilling renewal of the very foundations of trade and asset management.

NFTs

Non-Fungible Tokens (NFTs) represent a significant shift in the digital world, like unique digital collectibles. Imagine owning a digital trading card, a piece of artwork, or a unique musical composition – that's the essence of an NFT. Each NFT is distinct, possessing a digital certificate akin to a signature, which authenticates and establishes ownership. This certificate is stored on a blockchain, ensuring the authenticity and uniqueness of each NFT and safeguarding against counterfeiting.

For example, if a high-end brand like Dolce & Gabbana were to release a digital wearable for a metaverse as an NFT, the authenticity of this item could be verified through its blockchain contract. This verification process ensures that the item is not a counterfeit but an original piece from the brand. Such digital wearables can be purchased as NFTs and used as avatars in certain metaverses.

NFTs have garnered significant interest from artists and creators as a novel medium for selling their work. When an artist sells a piece of digital art or music as an NFT, they can continue to earn from it through royalties, receiving a percentage of sales each time the NFT is resold. This model provides a continuous revenue stream, as they would for receiving royalties for a song or artwork.

Beyond financial benefits, NFTs offer a platform for unrestricted creative expression. Artists can venture beyond conventional categories, exploring limitless possibilities in their creative endeavors. Once an artwork is recorded on the blockchain, it becomes a permanent, uncensorable part of the digital ledger.

The music industry is also experiencing a renaissance through NFTs. Musicians can release special tracks or albums as NFTs, allowing fans to own unique pieces of musical history. NFTs can also carry different licenses, such as theatrical or commercial usage rights, streamlining the process for purchasing and re-selling licensed music. This efficiency benefits both artists and consumers, simplifying the management of intellectual property rights.

The gaming industry is also enhancing their experience through using NFTs. Traditionally, in-game assets become obsolete with the release of a new game version, trapping players' investments in the outdated version. However, NFTs are changing this dynamic. They enable in-game assets to be persistently trackable and transferable, offering players the ability to resell their assets instead of facing a total loss when they cease playing. This means that special skins or outfits purchased for characters could, ideally, be used in future game iterations, enhancing the value and longevity of players' investments in the game.

NFTs are also redefining real-world applications, such as event ticketing. An NFT ticket to a concert or event is not just a pass but a collectible item. This innovation enhances the value and experience of attending events, allowing attendees to prove their attendance and retain a piece of history in their digital wallets.

For companies and marketers, NFTs offer valuable insights into consumer preferences and behaviors. By analyzing the contents of a wallet, businesses can tailor their products, services, and experiences to individual interests, without compromising personal identity.

Sharing and showcasing collections is another advantage of NFTs. Unlike physical collectibles that require physical presence for sharing, NFTs can be viewed and appreciated remotely through a wallet address. This accessibility fosters social connections and conversations around shared interests in art, music, and collectibles.

Blockchain technology offers a significant advantage to artists and inventors in establishing the originality of their creations. By recording their work on the blockchain with NFTs or similar types of tokens, they gain a verifiable timestamp, serving as concrete evidence of ownership and creation date. This feature of blockchain presents a compelling use case in the realm of patents, offering a reliable method to timestamp the inception and authorship of an invention or design. While it does not entirely displace the existing intellectual property system, blockchain provides a robust mechanism to substantiate claims of originality, enhancing the ability of creators to demonstrate that they were the first to develop their unique work of art or invention.

NFTs are revolutionizing the way artists, musicians, gamers, creators, and collectors share and monetize their work, blending art, technology, and finance in a unique and innovative way. Whether one is an art enthusiast, a music lover, gamer, or a collector of unique items, NFTs offer a new and exciting realm to explore and engage with.

Metaverses

The concept of Metaverses is a pivotal aspect of the web3 revolution, representing a digital realm where the boundaries of reality are redefined. These virtual environments, accessible via computers or VR headsets, offer a supreme level of immersion, allowing users to experience a world where the only limit is their imagination.

Central to the appeal of Metaverses is the unparalleled freedom of expression they offer. Users can craft and customize their avatars in extraordinary ways, transcending the constraints of the physical world. Whether it's adopting fantastical features like pink hair and elf ears, or alternating between a robotic and wizardly appearance, the Metaverses provide a platform for boundless self-expression.

In these digital landscapes, fashion takes on a new dimension, going beyond mere attire to become a form of statement and artistic expression. Users can put on outfits that defy the laws of physics, change hues based on emotions, or even exhibit luminescence. This opens up exciting avenues for fashion enthusiasts and designers, allowing them to set trends and create styles that are unattainable in the real world.

However, Metaverses offer more than just aesthetic customization. They provide experiences that are impossible in the physical realm. From the freedom of flight to exploring oceanic depths without the need for scuba gear, these virtual worlds enable users to live out their most fantastical dreams and aspirations.

One of the most captivating features of Metaverses is the ability to virtually 'travel' to diverse global destinations without leaving one's home. Users can wander through Parisian streets, ascend the Himalayas, or unwind on a Fijian beach, all within moments. Each virtual locale boasts its unique theme and atmosphere, offering endless exploration and adventure.

Moreover, Metaverses serve as a dynamic platform for cultural exchange. Users can participate in global events, festivals, and ceremonies, fostering a virtual cultural exchange program. This immersive approach allows for a deeper understanding and appreciation of diverse cultures and traditions.

For enthusiasts of fiction, Metaverses present the opportunity to step into the realms of beloved books, movies, or games. Imagine attending a wizarding school or joining forces with iconic superheroes. These experiences, which once resided in the realm of fantasy, are now tangible realities in the Metaverses.

Metaverses are canvases for creativity, hubs for cultural immersion, and playgrounds for the imagination. Whether one's interests lie in fashion, travel, or fantasy, Metaverses offer a universe of possibilities, epitomizing the transformative potential of the web3 revolution.

DApps

A Decentralized Application (DApp) is a software application that runs on a distributed computing system, often utilizing blockchain technology. Unlike traditional applications, which run on centralized servers, DApps operate on a peer-to-peer network, typically of nodes provided by blockchain infrastructure. This decentralized nature ensures that DApps are resistant to censorship, have reduced points of failure, and are more accessible, as there is no central server that can be targeted, shut down, or restrict access.

The need for DApps arises from the desire to promote greater transparency, security, integrity, and accessibility in various digital interactions and transactions. By leveraging blockchain technology, DApps provide an immutable record of transactions, ensuring that data cannot be tampered with once recorded. This is particularly beneficial in areas like finance, where trust and transparency are paramount. Additionally, DApps can facilitate smart contracts, which automatically execute transactions when predefined conditions are met, further reducing the need for intermediaries and lowering transaction costs.

Moreover, DApps empower users by giving them full control over their data and transactions, as opposed to traditional applications where user data can be controlled and used by the service provider. This aspect is crucial in an era where data privacy and security are major concerns. Furthermore, DApps are inherently more accessible as they are not bound by the geographical or jurisdictional limitations often associated with centralized servers and platforms. This global accessibility ensures that anyone with an internet connection can participate, making DApps particularly valuable in regions with limited access to traditional banking or online services. DApps represent a shift towards a more decentralized, transparent, secure, and accessible digital ecosystem, addressing many of the limitations and trust issues associated with traditional, centralized applications.

| 6 |

Preface to the Story

This story is inspired by true events and is the interpretation of the story in the way I saw it happen. Some parts of the story may be left out as it is unrelated to this topic. Names were also changed to protect the innocent. The story is more about learning the context of how everything fits together as well as seeing the dynamics of power. It offers a viewpoint through the lens of a Web3 frontier. Also, as a primer to the story, I will be giving an example of the Stereotypes and web3 roles comparing them to what roles they would play in the Wild Wild West. If you are interested in Decentralization and how DAOs operate and web3, then you will be interested in the story.

The Stereotypes and how they fit the Wild Wild West

The Bitcoin Maximalist

Bitcoin Maximalists, with their firm belief in the supremacy of Bitcoin over other cryptocurrencies, closely resemble the Catholic Church Priests of the Wild West. These maximalists assert that other digital currencies are superfluous or even harmful. They are often vocal about their convictions, engaging in debates and discussions, defending Bitcoin's superiority at every turn. They wholeheartedly believe that Bitcoin embodies the quintessential vision of what a decentralized currency should be. For many, this dedication borders on reverence, with Satoshi Nakamoto, the pseudonymous creator of Bitcoin, often being held in an almost worshipful regard.

On the frontier of the Wild West, Catholic Church Priests held significant sway, establishing and maintaining order in expanding towns. They stood as the community's moral compass, imparting teachings from the Bible and guiding their congregation with unwavering faith. Just as these priests resisted other religious influences they deemed heretical, Bitcoin Maximalists reject any cryptocurrency propositions that deviate from their Bitcoin-centered vision. Priests in the Wild West ventured great lengths to construct churches and propagate their faith, defending it against any perceived threats.

Drawing parallels, just as Bitcoin Maximalists champion the dominance of Bitcoin in the realm of cryptocurrencies, the Catholic Church Priests of yore staunchly defended their faith, resisting external influences that conflicted with their doctrine.

Both groups perceived themselves as guardians of a "truth". While Bitcoin Maximalists envision Bitcoin as the pioneering torchbearer of decentralized finance and revere its creator, the priests viewed Catholicism as the unerring faith. Amidst the fervent debates and confrontations, both groups ardently defended their beliefs. And just as the priests were instrumental in sowing the seeds of order in the chaotic terrains of the Wild West, Bitcoin Maximalists envisage themselves as the heralds of a decentralized future in the tumultuous world of cryptocurrencies.

The Web3 Purists

Web3 Purists and their deep-seated belief in the overarching promise of decentralization can be likened to the Protestant priests of the Wild West. While the Bitcoin Maximalists, alike to Catholic Church Priests, are unwavering in their commitment to a singular vision, Web3 Purists, much like the Protestant priests, embrace a broader perspective.

In the ever-evolving landscape of the crypto world, Web3 Purists champion the ideals of a decentralized internet, believing in its potential to revolutionize traditional systems. Their belief is not confined to just Bitcoin; they are willing to acknowledge and embrace the potential of various blockchains that align with the core ethos of decentralization.

Parallelly, in the Wild West, Protestant priests brought with them a reformed vision of Christianity. They sought to distance themselves from the centralized authority of the Catholic Church, emphasizing a personal connection to the divine and individual interpretation of scriptures. They believed in the core tenets of Christianity but were open to diverse practices and teachings within that framework.

Just as the Protestant priests were open to a range of interpretations and practices under the broad umbrella of Christianity, Web3 Purists acknowledge the expansive horizon of blockchains beyond just Bitcoin. They uphold the sanctity of decentralization, yet remain open to the myriad possibilities that different blockchains present, much like the Protestant priests who, while adhering to the core teachings, welcomed a plurality of perspectives.

The Trolls

Trolls in the modern digital and crypto sphere find their counterpart in the Wild West's agitators and rabble-rousers. These are individuals who thrive on causing disruptions, sowing discord, and often act out of the sheer joy of watching chaos unfold or to divert attention for various reasons.

In the online world, especially in crypto communities, trolls frequent forums, social media platforms, and chat groups. Their primary aim is to provoke, spread misinformation, create divisions, or simply to get a rise out of genuine enthusiasts and experts. They might spread FUD (Fear, Uncertainty, Doubt) about a particular cryptocurrency, misleading new investors or causing panic sales. Their motivations can vary from personal amusement to deliberate attempts to manipulate the market or tarnish reputations.

Back in the Wild West, towns and saloons had their own troublemakers. These individuals would stir up conflicts, spread rumors, or incite bar brawls for various reasons. Some did it for entertainment in an otherwise hard and monotonous life, while others might have had ulterior motives like diverting attention from some other misdeeds or targeting specific individuals or groups. Their actions could lead to heightened tensions in already volatile settings.

Both trolls and Wild West agitators thrive on chaos and reactions from those around them. The digital trolls hide behind the anonymity that the internet offers, much like how the vastness and lawlessness of the Wild West provided cover for its rabble-rousers. While the settings and mediums differ, the essence of their actions remains similar: disrupt, provoke, and revel in the ensuing chaos.

The Shillers

Shillers in the crypto space are much like certain journalists during the Wild West era. They often operate in the gray area of influence and self-interest, potentially leading audiences astray for personal or collective gains.

In the crypto ecosystem, shillers are individuals or entities that aggressively promote and hype up specific cryptocurrencies, not necessarily based on the coin's fundamental value but more on the potential for quick profits. This promotion can lead to artificially inflated prices, where unsuspecting investors buy into the hype. Once the price is pumped up sufficiently, those behind the scheme dump their holdings, leading to a rapid decline in the coin's value and leaving late investors at a loss.

Besides being behind the hyping of specific cryptocurrencies, they also can play a role in creating a FUD (Fear, Uncertainty, Doubt) movement that rapidly decreases the prices of the selected cryptocurrency. This gives them a chance to buy in at lower prices.

In the Wild West, some journalists and publishers wielded significant influence over the public's perception through their newspapers and stories. Not always bound by ethics or accuracy, these journalists occasionally sensationalized events or spread rumors, influencing migrations, investments, or perceptions for personal gain or at the behest of powerful entities. They could sway public opinion and actions based on the stories they chose to tell, or the way they framed certain events, much like shillers can influence public investment decisions in the crypto world.

It's worth noting, however, that while these comparisons hold, not all journalists of the Wild West were involved in such practices, just as not everyone promoting a cryptocurrency is involved in a pump and dump scheme. But the power of influence and narrative can be wielded in both beneficial and harmful ways, whether in the untamed frontiers of the Wild West or the digital landscapes of cryptocurrencies.

The Miners

Miners in the crypto realm can be likened to the gold miners during the Wild West era. Their roles, motivations, and impacts draw several parallels between the two domains.

In the vast digital landscape of cryptocurrencies, miners play a crucial role in validating and recording transactions on a blockchain. They employ powerful computer systems to solve complex mathematical problems. Once these problems are solved, a new block is added to the blockchain, and miners are rewarded with cryptocurrency for their efforts. This process, while ensuring the security and integrity of transactions, also introduces new coins into the system.

During the Wild West era, gold miners ventured into uncharted territories, driven by the allure of discovering gold. They invested time, resources, and often their life savings, setting up mining operations in the hopes of unearthing valuable gold ores. These endeavors not only contributed to personal wealth but also played a pivotal role in the economic expansion of the region, attracting settlers, businesses, and investments.

Just as gold miners were essential in extracting valuable resources from the earth and spurring economic growth, crypto miners are integral in maintaining the integrity of blockchain networks and facilitating the circulation of new tokens. Both groups work in environments characterized by competition, where the quest is to be the first to uncover value, be it in the form of a gold nugget or the solution to a cryptographic problem.

Furthermore, as the gold rush led to the development of towns, infrastructure, and communities around mining areas, the crypto mining boom has led to the creation of mining pools, advancements in computing technology, and the establishment of regulations around cryptocurrency operations.

Essentially, the miners of the crypto world, with their computational rigs and algorithms, mirror the spirit and drive of the gold miners of the Wild West, each pivotal in their respective landscapes, forging paths and shaping the future.

The Stakers

Stakers in the crypto realm are individuals who lock up a certain amount of their cryptocurrency to support the operations of a blockchain network. By doing so, they earn rewards, usually in the form of additional tokens. This process, known as staking, is a fundamental component of Proof-of-Stake (PoS) and some other consensus mechanisms which aim to achieve network security and consensus without the intense energy requirements of Proof-of-Work (like in Bitcoin mining).

Depicting a resemblance to the Wild West, stakers can be likened to the farmers or homesteaders who would stake a claim on a piece of land, cultivate it, and reap the benefits of their labor over time.

In the uncharted territories of the Wild West, securing a piece of land and committing to its development was a significant investment. Farmers would clear the land, plant crops, and then wait for the harvest. Their investment wasn't just in the form of the initial claim, but also in the time, effort, and resources they poured into the land to make it productive.

Similarly, in the crypto ecosystem, stakers invest by locking up their tokens, effectively betting on the success and security of the network. They contribute to the network's stability and, in return, earn rewards over time. Just as the farmer's commitment helps in the growth and sustenance of the land, the staker's commitment ensures the robustness and security of the block-chain network.

In theory, both the stakers, and Wild West farmers symbol-ize a form of long-term commitment and belief in the potential of an asset, be it land or a blockchain. Their investment, time, and patience often yield returns, making their endeavors worth-while in their respective frontiers.

The Developers

Developers in the crypto realm can be likened to the pioneers and architects of the Wild West. Both groups have been instru-mental in building foundational elements, laying out infrastruc-ture, and shaping the direction of their respective landscapes.

In the crypto world, developers are the backbone of the industry. They design, build, and maintain the various block-chains, smart contracts, and decentralized applications that drive this new frontier of finance and technology. Their work goes beyond just code – they conceptualize and implement the visions and principles of decentralization, privacy, and trustless transactions. Every blockchain, every token, every decentralized platform exists due to the tireless efforts of these developers.

In the context of the Wild West, pioneers and architects played a similar foundational role. As settlers moved west-ward in search of new opportunities, these individuals were at the forefront of establishing new towns, laying railway tracks, constructing buildings, and more. They envisioned the layout and structure of towns, ensuring that there was order amidst the chaos. These builders determined how communities would grow and evolve, setting down the groundwork for generations to come.

Developers were much like the pioneering architects of the Wild West. They are visionaries who lay the framework for new worlds. In the vast, untamed realm of cryptocurrencies, developers forge paths, build infrastructures, and craft the very tools and platforms that allow for growth and evolution. Similarly, in the expansive and rugged landscapes of the Wild West, architects and pioneers planned, constructed, and established the foundations for thriving communities. Both groups, in their respective domains, have been instrumental in translating vision into reality, turning wild frontiers into landscapes of opportunity and innovation.

The WAGMI Collective

"WAGMI," an acronym for "We're All Going to Make It," is a popular phrase within the cryptocurrency community, embodying a spirit of optimism and collective success. It's often used to express a shared belief in the future success of cryptocurrencies as a whole, or in the potential of specific projects or investments within this space. The term captures the essence of communal hope and the conviction that, despite the ups and downs of the market, the community will ultimately thrive.

In the context of the Wild West, the equivalent of "WAGMI" people might be the optimistic settlers and prospectors. These individuals ventured into the unknown with a shared belief in a brighter future. They were driven by the hope of prosperity, be it through discovering gold, securing fertile land for farming, or starting a new life in a land of opportunities. Their collective optimism was a driving force behind the expansion and development of the West.

Like the "WAGMI" enthusiasts in the crypto world, these settlers and prospectors faced significant risks and uncertainties. The volatility of the gold market, the harshness of untamed lands, and the myriad other challenges of frontier life were akin to the fluctuating fortunes of the crypto market. Yet, their steadfast belief in a better future, the notion that they were all in it together and that their endeavors would eventually bear fruit, kept them going.

Both the "WAGMI" people of the crypto community and the optimistic pioneers of the Wild West share this unifying spirit of hope and perseverance. In both realms, it's this communal optimism that often acts as a buffer against uncertainties and challenges, fueling progress and driving individuals to push beyond the immediate hurdles towards a vision of collective success.

The Whales

In the crypto sphere, "whales" are individuals or entities that hold a significant amount of a specific cryptocurrency. Their actions and decisions can profoundly influence market dynamics. Similarly, in the Wild West, there were influential magnates or barons who held significant sway over specific industries or regions, using their vast resources to impact local economies, politics, and developments.

In the world of cryptocurrencies, whales have the power to move the market dramatically. A single large purchase or sale by a whale can cause sharp price increases or decreases. Given their substantial holdings, their investment strategies, or mere rumors about their potential moves, can create waves of speculation among smaller investors. Their influence is so pronounced that many in the crypto community closely watch the activities of known whale accounts, trying to glean insights or anticipate market moves.

During the days of the Wild West, tycoons, particularly those in the railroad, cattle, and mining industries, held analogous power. They owned vast swaths of land, controlled major business enterprises, and had the capital to fund large-scale projects. Their decisions about where to lay railroad tracks, where to set up mining operations, or how to manage cattle drives could significantly impact local economies, determine the prosperity of towns, and influence migration patterns. Just as crypto communities watch whales, people in the Wild West would keep a close eye on these magnates, knowing that their actions could bring fortune or famine.

Drawing a comparison: just as whales in the cryptocurrency markets have the power to shape market dynamics with their vast holdings and strategic moves, the magnates of the Wild West used their resources and influence to mold the socioeconomic landscapes of their time. Both groups, by virtue of their disproportionate resources, wield significant power, and their actions can have ripple effects that impact many others in their respective ecosystems.

The Simps

In the crypto community, the term "Simp" has taken on a unique connotation, referring to individuals who display an unwavering and often uncritical loyalty to certain key figures or groups within the space. This term is typically used to describe someone who is excessively devoted to someone else, often to the point of being overly subservient or sycophantic, in hopes of gaining favor or some form of return. Often, it refers to a man who is trying to win over a woman. However, in web3 gender is irrelevant for this term; it's basically another word for a crony in the negative context of cronyism.

In the broader context of web3, this kind of allegiance goes beyond mere financial investment; it becomes an integral part of their identity and belief system. These individuals are often highly active in online forums and social media, zealously promoting their chosen leader or group. Their enthusiasm can sometimes blind them to any criticism or skepticism, leading to a somewhat one-sided perspective.

This phenomenon often involves aligning with the market's most influential players, known as 'whales.' These whales hold substantial stakes in cryptocurrencies and have the power to influence market trends significantly. Simps are drawn to the success and influence of these whales, often mimicking their investment strategies, and echoing their public opinions. They become vocal supporters of the whales' decisions and viewpoints, seeing their association with these influential figures as a validation of their own choices and beliefs in the cryptocurrency world.

This dynamic is reminiscent of the devoted followers in the Wild West, who would unwaveringly support charismatic leaders, whether they were pioneering town founders, influential entrepreneurs, or even notorious outlaws. Their loyalty was a key element in their leader's success. Whether it was about defending a claim or establishing a new community, their commitment was unwavering, and they rarely tolerated any criticism or opposition.

In the crypto world, Simps often mirror the actions and attitudes of the whales they admire, sometimes to the point of ignoring their own principles or the broader implications of their actions. This can create a challenging environment for anyone who opposes their admired leader. This dynamic highlights the significant influence that charismatic and powerful figures can wield, whether in the historical context of the Wild West or in the modern, ever-changing space of cryptocurrency markets.

The Degens

"Degens" is a colloquial term in the crypto and online gambling community, derived from the word "degenerate". In the crypto context, it often refers to individuals who take extremely high risks, speculating on new, untested, or highly volatile projects, hoping for rapid and significant returns. Their approach is typically characterized by a high-risk, high-reward mindset, often bordering on recklessness.

In the Wild West, the closest analog to the "Degens" might be the gamblers and fortune-seekers who flocked to the saloons and gambling dens, betting their hard-earned money or gold on games of chance. Much like the Degens of the crypto world, these individuals were driven by the allure of quick wealth, often staking significant sums on the turn of a card or the roll of dice.

Both groups share a penchant for high stakes and the thrill of the gamble. They're less deterred by potential losses than they are enticed by the possibility of substantial gains. For the crypto Degens, the digital landscape offers a vast array of tokens, projects, and platforms where fortunes can, in theory, be made overnight. Their Wild West counterparts found their adrenaline rush in the dimly-lit, smoky interiors of saloons, where the clink of coins and the thrill of the game promised riches or ruin.

The underlying theme connecting both is the pursuit of reward amidst uncertainty. While the tools and settings differ— digital tokens versus poker chips, online exchanges versus saloons—the essence remains: a high-stakes game where fortunes can be won or lost in the blink of an eye. Both the Degens and their Wild West counterparts embody the spirit of risk, reward, and the allure of the unknown.

The Vigilantes

Vigilantes in the context of the Wild West were individuals or groups that took the law into their own hands, often because they felt that formal law enforcement was inadequate, corrupt, or simply absent. These self-appointed enforcers would track down and punish wrongdoers based on their own sense of justice, sometimes acting with community support, and at other times, facing opposition for their methods and decisions.

In the realm of cryptocurrency and the broader digital space, "vigilantes" can be likened to white-hat hackers or community-led groups that seek to identify vulnerabilities, expose scams, or rectify injustices in the ecosystem. Much like their Wild West counterparts, these modern vigilantes often step in where they perceive official channels to be lacking or slow to act.

Both groups are driven by a sense of justice and a desire to protect their communities. Wild West vigilantes, faced with lawless territories and oftentimes corrupt or non-existent law enforcement, felt compelled to intervene directly, seeking retribution against outlaws or defending their towns. In the digital age, crypto vigilantes, aware of the scams, hacks, and fraudulent schemes that proliferate the space, endeavor to safeguard the community, either by responsibly disclosing vulnerabilities to projects or by publicly exposing bad actors.

However, the actions of both groups can also be controversial. While their intentions might be noble, the act of taking the law into one's own hands can sometimes lead to unintended consequences or the meting out of disproportionate justice. Just as vigilantes in the Wild West could sometimes misjudge or be overly harsh, crypto vigilantes might face criticism for their methods or for potential overreaches.

With that being said, the vigilantes of the Wild West and the digital defenders of the crypto space embody the spirit of grassroots justice and community protection. Acting outside of official channels, they highlight both the strengths and vulnerabilities inherent in their respective environments.

The DAO Drainers

"DAO Drainers" refers to those who exploit vulnerabilities in Decentralized Autonomous Organizations (DAOs). DAOs are organizations that operate based on pre-set rules encoded in blockchain smart contracts. While they hold the promise of decentralization and democratization, they're not immune to flaws or vulnerabilities in their code.

The most notorious instance of this was the 2016 DAO hack, where an individual or group took advantage of a loophole in the DAO's smart contract, draining millions of dollars worth of Ether, leading to a contentious hard fork in the Ethereum blockchain to recover the funds.

Comparatively, in the Wild West, we can liken the DAO drainers to the cunning bank or train robbers. These outlaws meticulously planned and executed heists, identifying vulnerabilities in banks' security or train routes to make away with large sums of money or precious cargo.

Both DAO drainers and Wild West robbers operate(ed) in environments characterized by new opportunities and rapid change. For the robbers of the Wild West, the expansion of railroads and the establishment of new banks in burgeoning towns presented lucrative targets. In the crypto realm, the growth of DeFi platforms and DAOs presents both opportunities for genuine innovation and targets for those with nefarious intentions.

The common thread between these two groups is their ability to spot vulnerabilities in emerging systems and exploit them for significant gain. While the tools, tactics, and terrains differ, the underlying motivation and the act of capitalizing on weaknesses remain consistent. Both groups represent challenges that new frontiers face, requiring evolving defenses and governance to ensure safety and trust.

The Rug Pullers

In the crypto world, "rug pullers" are individuals or groups that scam investors by suddenly withdrawing all their deposited funds from a decentralized platform, often after hyping up a project or token. Once they've amassed enough investments, they disappear, leaving investors with worthless tokens or locked funds.

Drawing a parallel to the Wild West, rug pullers are reminiscent of the con artists and swindlers of that era. These opportunists would arrive in new towns or settlements, often peddling fake medicines, counterfeit gold claims, or other too-good-to-be-true schemes. They'd create a buzz, entice locals with grand stories and promises, and once they had their money, they'd vanish, leaving behind a trail of cheated victims.

Both rug pullers and Wild West con artists thrive on the excitement of new frontiers – whether it's the untapped territories of the West or the burgeoning world of decentralized finance. Their success lies in the uncertainty and lack of regulation in these areas, allowing them to exploit unsuspecting individuals before making a quick exit.

| 7 |

The Story

The story unfolds in 2016 as BlockBaron receives an introduction to Bitcoin from a close friend named Raskalnikov. BlockBaron was taught about the intricacies of this digital currency and the mechanisms that drive it. Prior to this, BlockBaron heard the echoes of Mt. Gox's epic failure leading to bankruptcy. BlockBaron despite hearing about this, decided to listen to his friend. Raskalnikov guided him through the creation of his first paper wallet, emphasizing the importance of noting down the private key and never saving it on a computer, as this would only entice hackers. The private key is essential, as it is the sole means of transferring Bitcoin from the wallet; without it, access is impossible. BlockBaron wrote down his private key on a notecard.

Consider a private key as the key to a vault storing your money. It bears resemblance to a bank, where your funds are held and transactions are made on your behalf, but with a crucial difference—banks have full control over your money. While the public has grown to trust banks with their funds, Bitcoin and other cryptocurrencies embody a distrust towards any individual or entity having custody of the private key. Early adopters of cryptocurrency recognize that banks lend out deposited funds, ostensibly in exchange for safeguarding them. However, many cryptocurrency enthusiasts believe this system is flawed and vulnerable to collapse, with banks potentially shutting down and absconding with the deposits. While government insurance programs exist to mitigate such risks, they often rely on tax dollars from the country's citizens. Addressing such a crisis could necessitate increased taxes or inflation of the government's fiat currency, both of which harm citizens. To sidestep such issues, cryptocurrency holders prefer to take responsibility for their own private keys, maintaining control and ensuring security.

BlockBaron's journey into the world of cryptocurrency started with Bitcoin. After accumulating it for a few months, his curiosity led him to explore other digital currencies, leading him to BTC-e, a vibrant cryptocurrency trading platform that mirrored a Wall Street trading floor, particularly due to the presence of the troll box. This chat feature, situated beside the trading interface, became a battlefield for bitcoin maximalists and web3 purists, each fervently advocating for their preferred cryptocurrencies. Amidst this, there were the trolls, individuals with intentions of sowing fear, uncertainty, and doubt, spreading misinformation, and deriving enjoyment from the chaos they created.

BTC-e operated as a centralized exchange, requiring users to deposit funds into a wallet controlled by the platform—a common practice, but one necessitating trust. However, this era was rife with scammers creating illusions of trustworthiness, in a digital realm yet untouched by regulations and enforcement.

BlockBaron had amassed over 30 Ether (the currency of the Ethereum Protocol or Network), his preferred cryptocurrency, when suddenly, the FBI seized the domain and assets listed on the BTC-e platform. The authorities attributed this action to an international money laundering scheme and the alleged laundering of funds from the Mt. Gox hack. This incident served as a harsh lesson for BlockBaron, who saw all his funds seized, with only half eventually returned. The experience brought to life the saying, "Not your keys, not your crypto," a sentiment echoing from the legendary incident at Mt. Gox in 2014. At that time, Mt. Gox, the infamous Bitcoin Exchange responsible for handling 70% of all Bitcoin transactions worldwide, suffered a massive theft from their hot wallet.

This experience prompted BlockBaron to explore decentralized exchanges (also known as DEXs), platforms where users maintain full control and custody of their crypto, as they trade directly from wallets to which they hold the private keys. While trading from one's own wallet offers benefits, it also necessitates managing gas fees (blockchain network usage fees) and entering the private key—a case-sensitive alphanumeric code—each time. Despite not storing the private key on a computer, a blackhat hacker could potentially keylog the entries to access it.

Every transaction on the blockchain necessitates a signature from the wallet in use. Traditionally, this would mean manually entering the private key for each transaction. However, the introduction of Metamask, a browser extension that stores the private key locally, marked a significant change. This convenience, however, renders the wallet "hot" and vulnerable, as the private key is stored within an application or computer file, contrasting with the security of a "cold" wallet, like a paper wallet where the private key is written down. BlockBaron was convinced that a more optimal solution must exist.

A hardware wallet interfaces with the Metamask application in a unique way; while Metamask facilitates transactions, it doesn't store the private key of the hardware wallet. Typically, Metamask would use a stored private key to request a signature by having the user click a button, but with a hardware wallet, the process is different. When a signature is requested, the hardware wallet must be connected to the computer, and a physical button on the wallet pressed, allowing it to temporarily sign the transaction using the private key stored within. This adds a layer of security, preventing hackers without physical access to the hardware wallet from conducting unauthorized transactions or stealing funds. If someone were to physically acquire the hardware wallet, they would have only three attempts to enter the correct code before the device wipes all stored information. In such a scenario, the legitimate owner, armed with their recovery paper containing the necessary information, can still recover their funds. Recognizing these security benefits, BlockBaron decided to invest in his first hardware wallet, significantly bolstering the protection of his assets against unauthorized access.

Now armed with a hardware wallet and navigating through decentralized exchanges, BlockBaron encountered a plethora of new cryptocurrencies. These exchanges enabled a myriad of cryptocurrencies to be listed for trade, paving the way for numerous scammers to craft fraudulent cryptocurrencies, complete with deceptive websites, whitepapers, and roadmaps. These scammers established trading pairs to exploit fortune seekers who overlooked details or succumbed to the fear of missing out. By creating a trading pair of a fabricated crypto, boasting promised utility, with a valuable cryptocurrency like Ether, scammers could easily trade their worthless currency for one of substantial value. Once the exchange was made, they would vanish, only to re-emerge with a different identity and wallet, ready to repeat the scheme. This method proved to be highly lucrative for these unscrupulous individuals.

However, much of the credibility of these scammers was bolstered by shillers and fabricated news articles. While these shillers and influencers were not the founders of such fraudulent or poorly conceived projects, they would often invest in them before the public caught wind. The ensuing hype from influencers lent an air of credibility to numerous cryptocurrency projects, which promised revolutionary ideas but ultimately either collapsed or were never genuinely pursued by their founders. Nonetheless, it was the shillers and influencers who managed to sell at a profit, leaving the average investor holding the proverbial bag. These dubious cryptocurrencies proliferated, becoming like penny stocks, tantalizing with the prospect of substantial rewards if they proved successful.

Choosing the right cryptocurrency projects was challenging enough, but the added expense of network fees payable to miners made buying and exchanging cryptos even more daunting. This led BlockBaron and other crypto enthusiasts, weary of pursuing the latest cryptos with alluring yet unattainable roadmaps, to explore alternative avenues for earning crypto.

Many turned their attention to mining cryptocurrencies, sparking a gold rush in crypto mining. Soon, acquiring graphic processing units (GPUs), or graphics cards as they are sometimes called, became exceedingly difficult. Typically, GPUs are sought after by gamers and individuals requiring high video processing capabilities for their computers. However, during this crypto mining boom, even recreational computer builders struggled to find available graphics cards, with some units fetching up to ten times their regular price due to the unprecedented demand. These GPUs were the equivalent of pickaxes during a gold rush —indispensable tools for anyone looking to mine crypto.

BlockBaron allocated a significant portion of his crypto gains to construct his own mining rig. For someone inexperienced in building computers, this was no small feat. Fortunately, a friend, known by the nickname Bananas, offered his assistance. Bananas earned his moniker during an extensive hike on the Appalachian Trail, journeying from Georgia to Maine. Unfortunately, his adventure was cut short in Vermont when he contracted Lyme disease. His trail name, Bananas, originated from his fellow hikers, who found his fervent visions of anarchy quite unconventional, deeming his ideas as "bananas."

In any case, Bananas owned a mining rig himself. A rig is essentially a computer equipped with multiple GPUs, specifically designed for mining cryptocurrency. Many rigs were barebones, featuring a motherboard, CPU, and risers connected to several openly mounted GPUs. Bananas possessed extensive knowledge in assembling such a rig. Having six GPUs operating on a single computer motherboard is not standard and is relatively uncommon. However, with a minor adjustment to the motherboard's BIOS—voilà!—BlockBaron's mining rig was complete. With Bananas' assistance, BlockBaron gained valuable insights and knowledge.

In crypto mining, monitoring electricity consumption is crucial to compare the operational costs of the mining rig against the earnings in cryptocurrency. About six months into his venture, BlockBaron found that the prices of Ether, which he had been mining, had fallen below a level that made mining profitable; it became more economical to simply buy the cryptocurrency. Consequently, he shut down his rig. While waiting for a potential resurgence, BlockBaron noticed a decline in GPU prices. Deciding to mitigate further losses on the hardware investment, he chose to sell his rig. Although this venture yielded some profit, it wasn't particularly noteworthy.

The Bear Market

The bear market presented BlockBaron with a golden opportunity to refine his cryptocurrency portfolio. During this period, characterized by falling prices and often pessimism in the market, BlockBaron took the chance to reassess and consolidate his investments in cryptocurrencies. This was an ideal time for him to sift through his holdings, retaining those projects with solid fundamentals and potential for growth, while discarding any that had shown signs of faltering fundamentals or other underlying issues.

Besides trimming the fat, this strategic move during the bear market provided BlockBaron with valuable insights into which cryptocurrencies were resilient enough to withstand the market's downturns. By closely observing how different projects weathered the storm, he could identify those with the strength and stability to survive and thrive beyond the bear market.

Another silver lining of a bear market is its tendency to cleanse the ecosystem of scammers. As the market contracts and the overall size and value of investments decrease, the lucrative allure that attracts scammers diminishes. This natural filtering effect can be seen as a form of market hygiene. The reduced profitability not only discourages new scammers from entering but also forces existing ones to either adapt (often by moving to other, more lucrative markets) or cease operations. For Block-Baron and genuine investors in the market, this is a period of relative respite, where they can operate with a slightly reduced risk of encountering fraudulent schemes.

Moreover, a bear market can serve as a reality check, prompting investors to become more cautious and discerning. This heightened vigilance further contributes to an environment that is less hospitable to scammers. Essentially, while bear markets are often viewed negatively due to their impact on investment values, they also play a crucial role in purging the market of some of its more predatory elements, thereby contributing to a healthier and more sustainable ecosystem in the long run.

When the market eventually shifted into a bull phase, characterized by rising prices and generally positive sentiment, BlockBaron was well-prepared. His portfolio, now streamlined and focused on high-potential projects, was primed to take full advantage of the upswing. This strategic positioning meant that as the market's tide turned, BlockBaron was ready to ride the wave of the next bull market, potentially reaping the benefits of his careful planning and foresight during the more challenging bear market period.

NFTs – a new journey

While BlockBaron was engrossed in mining with his crypto rig, Bananas was already exploring new horizons. He continued mining but had his sights set on the latest craze—CryptoKitties, having acquired a few himself. This venture was one of the pioneering NFT projects. Each CryptoKitty is represented as an ERC-721 token or an NFT (Non-Fungible Token), endowed with distinct features. These unique attributes are encoded as the CryptoKitty's phenotype and genotype, essentially the genetic information determining its appearance and other traits, integrated directly into the ERC-721 token's code. The myriad combinations of phenotypes and genotypes result in four billion possible CryptoKitties, ensuring the uniqueness of each one in the world.

Indeed, CryptoKitties were simply digital art pieces that can be "bred," collected, and traded, but they represented one of the first applications of this technology. Their popularity was so immense that they congested the Ethereum Network, causing delayed transactions and skyrocketing gas fees. The craze reached such heights that one CryptoKitty even sold for over $117,000. At the time, BlockBaron struggled to comprehend how a jpeg image on the blockchain could command such a staggering value.

Like all bubbles, this one too burst, leading to a decline in prices. During the subsequent 2-3 years of market stagnation, often referred to as the bear market, the landscape cleared, allowing genuine developers to build and the fraudulent projects to wither away. Scammers typically emerge during market bubbles, finding it easier to conceal flaws amidst the prevailing hype and fear of missing out. Consequently, the bear market significantly diminished the incentives for scammers, driving away most of the less sophisticated ones. This period helped distinguish between projects that were genuinely focused on their roadmap and utility, and those primarily concerned with the value of their cryptocurrency.

Many traders and enthusiasts often overlook the benefits of a bear market. It is during these times that true value and honesty come to the forefront, fostering community building. Identifying honest investments with intrinsic utility becomes more straightforward. Developers work on enhancing the code, leading to better technology and numerous advancements. For instance, with the rising cost of electricity, many blockchains transitioned from mining to staking, reflecting the adaptability and evolution within the sector.

In a proof-of-stake system, participants, known as "validators," lock up a specified amount of cryptocurrency or crypto tokens—their "stake"—in a smart contract on the blockchain. In return, they have the opportunity to validate new transactions and earn rewards. However, should they incorrectly validate fraudulent or inaccurate data, they risk losing part or all their stake as a penalty. Those who chose to stake were typically long-term investors with faith in the enduring value of that cryptocurrency chosen. During this period, BlockBaron committed to staking Ether, pledging to keep it staked for two years or more.

As the bear market began to wane, new technologies started to surface, with Metaverses and NFTs becoming the center of attention. While Metaverses aren't necessarily reliant on blockchain technology, many are integral to the decentralized movement advocating for freedom. The thrill of self-expression and the ability to assume various personas depending on the world or realm one inhabits are significant draws. In the Metaverse, individuals have the freedom to become whatever they envision.

NFTs played a pivotal role in establishing ownership of various assets in the Metaverse, while also possessing their own unique utility. They symbolized a surge in freedom of expression, ownership, monetization, authenticity, and appreciation. The trend of adopting NFTs as profile pictures gained momentum, giving birth to communities of like-minded individuals united by artwork that resonated with their identities. Not only was this artwork authenticated by the blockchain but being part of certain communities or owning NFTs from specific collections also brought exclusive benefits.

NFTs opened up possibilities for a myriad of items—ranging from marriage certificates, digital baseball cards, and real estate deeds, to event tickets, access passes, and Metaverse wearables—to be bought, sold, traded, and/or recorded on the blockchain. This development paved the way for boundless opportunities. Being part of an NFT community, where members largely share similar values aligned with the brand of the NFT project, introduced the concept of governance for many people. Many NFT projects empowered their communities to make decisions on the project's behalf, typically operating on a principle where one NFT equaled one vote. Consequently, owning more NFTs from a particular collection granted an individual greater voting power. This rise in community building and roadmap direction led to the formation of Decentralized Autonomous Organizations (DAOs).

However, it's important to note that NFTs weren't the pioneers in evolving into DAOs. As communities around cryptocurrencies and NFT collections emerged, the decentralization of power was envisioned as a revolutionary step, allowing investors to influence the direction of the project. This shift marked the onset of chaos. With the freedom of decision-making power distributed among a diverse community, the dynamics of making choices and reaching consensus became a complex play of power.

In 2021, the NFTs came back in a bigger wave of euphoria. This time it wasn't only a few projects like CryptoKitties. It was filled with massive amounts of artwork and profile pictures NFTs. While you buy into these collections of art, every single NFT is one of a kind. Even without knowing much about NFTs, many people heard about the Bored Ape Yacht Club. This is a NFT collection of Apes depicted as different characters. While there were 10,000 apes in that collection, every Bored Ape was unique. These became a status symbol in the Web3 space eventually spreading to celebrities and other wealthy individuals. It is more than just artwork, they own the commercial IP rights of their character and they could essentially do whatever they want with it. It's almost as if you were part of a brand that was recognizable, but yet unique to your own character.

The Bored Ape Yacht Club brought in so much hype into the Web3 space. This euphoric wave in the NFT industry resulted in a 24.9 Billion Dollar Sales Volume in 2021 according to DappRadar. During this phase, it was brand knew, so it was easy to get fooled or rug pulled. BlockBaron bought into a few projects that copied the fundamentals of the Bored Ape Yacht Club, but was rugged (rug-pulled) by the founders of those projects pretty quickly. It was almost as if it was a cash grab.

The founders of these NFT projects typically made promises for some of the proceeds to support their community who bought into their art. This would help drive good deals for the community. An example of this was RTFKT (pronounced "artifact") who was a fashion NFT collection that wanted to bridge the gap between digital and physical world. Nike, Inc. ended up acquiring RTFKT. This is what good NFT project founders were capable of.

Other NFT Projects ended up created Decentralized Autonomous Organizations (DAOs) as the founders who created these NFT collections, wanted to leave the community with decision making power over those funds. After BlockBaron got rugged by those NFT projects which relied on the founders to act on their promises, BlockBaron chose to start looking at NFT projects that created DAOs.

The Sacred Ones

BlockBaron ended up joining 2 different DAOs where he had a chance to play different roles of power, giving him a better understanding of the dynamics of power based on the role he played in that DAO. There was 2 he joined and was more active in, The Sacred Ones and DecentraWorld. Fundamentally, these had different ways to gain voting power. The Sacred Ones (TSO) would give you voting power based on how many NFTs you owned. Meanwhile, DecentraWorld would give you voting power based on how much of the cryptocurrency token called Aura you owned, NFT wearables, NFT Names, and NFT Meta-verse land parcels. Depending on the type of items your wallet held, each weighing differently in terms of voting power, that would give you a total amount of Voting Power owned.

The Sacred Ones (TSO) was an NFT project where mint-ers received artwork depicting Sacred Beings with different vices. Owning this artwork granted access to a community that played a role in guiding its direction. While not a true DAO, it functioned in a similar manner. The structure was such that the Founder's Organization, known as MetaCrust, would exe-cute the wishes and decisions of the community. Predominantly rooted in gaming, this community's activities revolved around games that incorporated the artwork. Owners had the option to lease their artwork back to Metacrust where they would include the artwork in the game, and in return, they would receive royalties from the game's proceeds.

Within The Sacred Ones community, BlockBaron held a prominent position as the top holder of the NFTs. This sig-nificant holding earned him the title of a "whale" among com-munity members. However, being a whale came with its own set of challenges. Every decision he made was closely watched and often critiqued by other community members. For ap-proximately a year and four months, BlockBaron collaborated with MetaCrust, striving to steer the project towards success. While every proposal had to be officially approved by the DAO,

BlockBaron's substantial holdings meant he could easily pass or veto any proposal, in contrast to the collective efforts of many community members. Despite his intentions, the community perceived BlockBaron's influence as a potential threat, leading to internal conflicts. This discord eventually played a significant role in the project's downfall. But to fully understand, it's essential to delve into the journey.

On Minting Day, BlockBaron acquired approximately 300 of The Sacred Ones NFTs out of the total collection of 6,666. This acquisition granted him voting power of 300. Initially, his voting weight was relatively balanced in comparison to other members. While many projects typically sell out within a day, this particular project seemed like an undiscovered treasure. Its limited visibility was attributed to minimal marketing, but its promise of royalties and a strong legal foundation added significant value. The team behind the project was perceived to be top-tier, with the involvement of a Vice President from a Nasdaq-listed company further bolstering its credibility. These factors fueled BlockBaron's optimism. However, as months rolled by, the project's initial promises began to wane, especially concerning the three games that were initially pledged to be developed.

David, one of the founders, communicated to BlockBaron that they required more time to fulfill their commitments. Wanting to give the founders an opportunity to deliver on their promises, BlockBaron took proactive steps to add value to the project during this waiting period. He played a pivotal role in expanding the community and elevating its visibility through various metaverse events, trending Twitter hashtags, working with MetaCrust for fresh media content for the community to share, and weekly community meetings. One of his stand-out contributions was a song, entirely produced by BlockBaron, that celebrated the project. This song highlighted the project's unique features and served as a marketing tool to encourage more mints. Despite the challenges, and prior to BlockBaron's efforts, the project managed to mint about 2,500 out of the total 6,666 NFTs.

BlockBaron's efforts in fostering the community garnered significant interest. His dedication was so profound that many mistook him for one of the project's founders. However, Block-Baron would always clarify that he was merely a passionate supporter and advocate. A year into his involvement, 4,000 of the NFTs had been minted, leaving around 2,600 still available. By this time, BlockBaron had personally minted approximately 900 NFTs. This was about 60 ETH worth which was approxi-mately $100k at the time. His relentless efforts in nurturing the community and shaping its culture played a crucial role in the increased minting. Of course, the broader community's presence was indispensable. The community stood to benefit financially from the mints and 10% of all game proceeds. It's evident that a significant portion of the project's funding was derived from the mints due to BlockBaron's contribution efforts towards community building.

As the days rolled on, envy began to creep into the com-munity. Many of BlockBaron's proposals and initiatives, once celebrated, were now taken for granted. His activities in an-other DAO, DecentraWorld, began to impact his reputation within The Sacred Ones community. Any conflicts or issues in DecentraWorld reverberated back to The Sacred Ones, casting a shadow over BlockBaron's standing. Whispered rumors and insinuations of BlockBaron's alleged malicious intentions began to circulate, painting him in an increasingly negative light. Actions that were once seen as benevolent were now perceived as power grabs, with some even likening him to a tyrant. Despite these perceptions, BlockBaron's intentions remained in favor of The Sacred Ones community.

However, the mounting tensions culminated in a community coup, where those who orchestrated the uprising replaced BlockBaron's leadership. Ironically, under the new leadership, the project eventually lost its momentum and faded away. The turn of events was a heavy blow to BlockBaron. His dedication was evident, having committed roughly 20 hours a week for over a year to the project. This outcome was extremely disheartening when you consider his monetary, emotional and time investments into The Sacred Ones NFTs.

The conflict that seeped into The Sacred Ones community, originating from DecentraWorld, began when BlockBaron took a stand against a whale he perceived as acting maliciously. BlockBaron, valuing integrity, identified what he believed to be a scam in its early stages within the DecentraWorld DAO. He noticed this whale's attempts to siphon off the DAO's funds and decided to confront the situation head-on. Here's how the saga unfolded.

The DAO Fund Drainers of DecentraWorld

One day, BlockBaron approached the Metatrailers, hoping they would promote the Sacred Ones' Grand Opening of their

Casino in DecentraWorld during one of their events. The Meta-trailers portrayed themselves as champions of the Decentra-World community, projecting an image of selflessness, altruism, and unwavering positivity. The Sacred Ones, always willing to support other communities within the DecentraWorld Meta-verse, found it natural to seek such collaborations. However, it's worth noting that the Metatrailers, despite their positive facade, stemmed from a project that didn't mint out, founded by an individual named Chris.

At that time, Chris was pursuing a substantial grant from the DecentraWorld DAO, amounting to $120k, with the intent of launching a DJ battle series within DecentraWorld. His proposal involved utilizing various venues within DecentraWorld and compensating numerous participants. Chris wanted the Sacred Ones to pay $350 for 1 shout out at their event. It's totally fair to ask for money for that, however that price was more than the cost of hiring a DJ. BlockBaron countered Chris with $50 for 1 shoutout with hopes he would accept. Chris declined.

That is all well and good as that is how consensual business works. However, as someone who is actively going for a grant of $120k and a shoutout that would essentially cost nothing is not a good look. Greed was clearly in the eyes of Chris. Chris was a great example of a snake oil salesman. He was good with charm and leading everyone to believe he had the miracle answer and was the king of web3. However, BlockBaron saw right through that.

BlockBaron started to dig further into Chris as he felt his moves were not very business savvy. A good businessman would not let a little drop in the bucket, ruin the potential of getting the whole bucket filled. Clearly, he was very short-sighted. After doing further digging, it appears Chris comes from a country that was underprivileged. You tend to see more scammers coming from those types of countries. Of course, there are scammers everywhere, but that was a caution flag for BlockBaron. However that wasn't enough to assume anything. However, BlockBaron believed that where you grow up and who you surround yourself with influences your behavior.

BlockBaron then dug further into Chris which resulted in finding out that prior to the Metatrailers, he had a previous NFT project called Muskology where they worship Elon Musk's accomplishments. This Muskology NFT project was based on a fetish of Elon Musk and promised all the investors that they would have a chance to win a limited edition of a Tequila bottle that Elon Musk released through Tesla. That project had many promises that couldn't be validated, even by its own holders. There's no transparent proof that it was ever sent to one of the Holders. This was another caution flag for BlockBaron. The art of this project was also subpar. All of these findings lead BlockBaron to believe that this was all a front to scam people out of their money.

Then it appears that shortly after Chris decided to create the Metatrailers and got wearables made in DecentraWorld that was almost an exact replica of the Telsa Bot. He would then give these to his members. After this research there were more minor things that BlockBaron found suspicious.

What BlockBaron couldn't understand is how a founder of 2 failed projects was able to influence a Chinese investor of DecentraWorld to delegate their Voting Power to him. This

Chinese investor had 1 million Voting Power in Decentra-World. This was a significant amount. MetaTrailers did not completely fail per se, but it did not sell out and it lacked major interest by NFT investors.

This voting power delegated to Chris was used as leverage to help other grants get passed even if they weren't good pitches to the DecentraWorld DAO. Chris didn't care about Decentra-World as a whole, he only cared about the funds that are owned by the DAO. He wanted a piece of those funds, so when he voted for everyone else's grant, they returned the favor. People in the legal profession call this *Quid Pro Quo* meaning something for something or doing favors with an expectation of getting something in return. In this case, Chris was expecting their vote in return which would result in his project getting grant money from the DecentraWorld DAO.

Grant Received by Metatrailers

Despite the glaring inconsistencies and potential conflicts of interest, the DecentraWorld's DAO approved the grant. Only 1% of Votes were against the Metatrailers' grant proposal. It almost passed unanimously. BlockBaron was one of the votes against it. He knew something was fishy about the grant.

BlockBaron felt compelled to alert the community and protect the DAO's funds from potentially being misused by someone with a questionable track record. Chris's past NFT project had failed to deliver on its promises, and his self-proclaimed credentials were dubious at best. Claims of being a doctor were debunked through Open-Source Intelligence (OSINT) research.

Moreover, his alleged affiliations as an angel investor for prominent web3 companies like Opensea and Ripple were also proven false, a fact Chris eventually admitted publicly on the Discord server. Such red flags are often telltale signs of scammers in the space.

The grant's breakdown also raised eyebrows. The proposed payments to DJs and venues didn't seem to align with the grant details listed, and there was a notable discrepancy in the allocation of funds. Furthermore, Chris's decision to make payments "off-chain" – outside the transparent realm of the blockchain where transactions couldn't be tracked – added to the skepticism.

The community began to question the grant's actual value, doubting its potential to attract new users and debating whether the proposed activities justified the grant's size. It became evident that the same objectives could likely be achieved at a fraction of the cost. Yet, the grant's structure, which involved disbursing small amounts to over 50 recipients, seemed to strategically incentivize these individuals to vote in favor of the grant, further complicating the situation.

In the web3 domain, where traditional verification methods like Know Your Customer (KYC) are absent, trust and reputation become paramount. Consistency in one's online identity is crucial to build and maintain influence. BlockBaron's efforts to highlight the red flags and discrepancies in Chris's claims were initially met with skepticism, largely because he hadn't yet established a strong reputation within the DecentraWorld's community. His intentions, though genuine, were misconstrued by many. In a twist of irony, instead of being lauded for his vigilance, BlockBaron faced backlash. He was even banned on Discord by DecentraWorld DAO Discord moderators, accused of spreading FUD, when in reality, he was trying to protect the community from potential deceit.

After some time, BlockBaron was reinstated in the Decentra-World DAO Discord, and he persisted in communicating his concerns. Despite being part of the 1% of the total voting power who voted against the Metatrailers' grant, representing only one of the four votes out of a total of 136, his dedication and evidence managed to sway the community. As a result, the grant's vesting contract to Metatrailers was halted, preventing the full disbursement of the originally approved $120k. In the end, Metatrailers received only around half of that amount, saving the DAO $60k. These funds remained available to further develop and enhance the DecentraWorld platform in the future. At this time, this is where Chris and other beneficiaries of this Grant, and their friends started to cause FUD around BlockBaron. They made him seem like he was the outcast. This eventually bled into The Sacred Ones DAO.

Following this incident, the DecentraWorld DAO proposed and voted to temporarily halt new grant requests, allowing the community to shift its focus to the active grants already in place. This decision provided much-needed relief, giving the community a few months to assess the situation without the continuous debates and disagreements that had been prevalent in the Discord. It was a period of reflection and recalibration, ensuring that the community could move forward with a more vigilant and unified approach.

Grant Number Two for Metatrailers

During this time of paused grants, Metatrailers were no-where to be found. Just when you think, the Metatrailers were done, they come back with another grant request soon after the pause period for grants. This time, they requested $180k for a similar DJ Battle series project.

With their second grant request, Metatrailers returned with heightened vigor. With a whopping 1 million voting power they already had, they leveraged their whale powers in the DecentraWorld DAO to form alliances behind the curtain. They collaborated to ensure their grants passed, irrespective of the broader community's sentiments. This system, orchestrated by Chris and the Metatrailers, appeared to exploit conflicts of interest to their advantage. By roping in smaller participants and promising them a slice of the grant, they secured their votes. This strategy not only ensured support for their own proposals but also created a reciprocal arrangement where these partici-pants would back proposals by other whales. The balance of power was being manipulated, sidelining genuine community interests.

Chris, the mastermind behind Metatrailers, employed a cun-ning strategy to mask his conflicts of interest. By leveraging multiple anonymous wallets, which many suspected were also under his control, he aimed to obfuscate his direct involve-ment. To further distance himself from direct voting on his own proposals, Chris introduced a separate DAO Voting system exclusively for Metatrailer NFT Holders. This system allowed them to collectively decide how to wield the significant 1 million Voting Power in DecentraWorld. On the surface, it appeared as a democratic process, giving the impression that it was "the Metatrailer community's choice." However, in reality, it was a clever ruse to divert attention from Chris's vested interests and present a facade of impartiality.

This was a unique way to exploit the DAO for funds. Essentially, Chris could sell his Metatrailer NFTs in exchange for his voting power, while also getting supporters to support his cause. It basically became a group of DAO drainers who would do each other favors to get funds from the DecentraWorld DAO. This was all under the illusion of it being his community, the Metatrailers voting in favor of proposals and he would simply act on their behalf. Meanwhile Chris owned majority of his Metatrailer NFTs through many wallets to disguise that it was truly him voting on this. Some people did take the bait in order to get their grant funded by the DecentraWorld DAO. Any person without morals would pay $100 to seize thousands.

BlockBaron, having faced backlash from the community in the past for being the bearer of unwelcome news, initially chose to distance himself from the ongoing events. However, as he observed the rapid depletion of the DAO's funds due to a series of questionable grants, he grew increasingly concerned. Chris, in collaboration with his network of influential allies, managed to siphon off over $750k from the DAO through various projects. These projects, often of questionable value, were consistently approved due to the voting power of this alliance of whales, further undermining the true spirit of decentralized governance.

In response to the unchecked actions of Chris and his allies, BlockBaron and a group of like-minded individuals formed the Orcas. Their primary aim was to uphold the core principles of web3 and act as a counterforce to the DAO-draining activities. However, their resistance inadvertently led to the rise of bureaucratic structures within the DecentraWorld DAO. The Revocations committee was established, and existing Squads and Committees gained more influence. Ironically, while the Orcas' intention was to preserve decentralization, their actions indirectly contributed to a centralization of power within the DAO. This highlighted the delicate balance of governance in decentralized systems, where the actions of a few can significantly impact the freedoms of the many.

Let the rules be created!

In the midst of the DecentraWorld DAO's restructuring, a "Code of Ethics" was being drafted, ostensibly to guide behavior and decision-making within the community. However, the architects behind these guidelines were simps, cronies, and the very bureaucrats aligned with the controversial actors. Instead of creating a framework that would genuinely promote ethical behavior and transparency, the rules appeared to be more about stifling dissent and curbing free speech. Notably absent from this code was any mention of "Conflict of Interest," a glaring omission that further underscored the skewed priorities of its drafters. Rather than addressing the root ethical concerns, the focus seemed to be on consolidating power and silencing potential whistleblowers.

The unfolding saga of DecentraWorld serves as a microcosm of the broader challenges facing the web3 space. As pioneers navigate the balance between decentralization's ideals and the practicalities of governance, the outcome remains uncertain. Will the community manage to uphold the foundational principles of web3, or will it succumb to a hybrid model, a "web 2.5", where only select principles are retained? Only time will tell. As with any frontier, the path forward is fraught with challenges, but it's the choices made during these pivotal moments that will shape the future of the digital realm.

BlockBaron's eventual ban from DecentraWorld's Discord and forum highlighted a paradox within the community. Despite its commitment to decentralization, the platform's enforcement rules leaned towards centralization. If a member's ideas upset someone, they faced a mute ranging from 24 hours to a week, a method alike to a digital "time-out." This approach seemed to contradict the ethos of the decentralization movement, which typically opposes censorship and champions the freedom of thought and open sharing of ideas.

This situation arose partly because platforms like Decentra-World and other DAOs rely on centralized communication tools like Discord or web forums. These platforms are overseen by moderators, introducing an element of centralization. When humans set and enforce rules, biases are almost inevitable, leading to a contradiction in a movement that aims to eliminate central control. This incident with BlockBaron underscored the challenges facing decentralized communities in maintaining their foundational principles while operating on inherently centralized platforms.

The Story Continues

While BlockBaron, has lost hope for DecentraWorld and The Sacred Ones, he hasn't lost hope for Web3. BlockBaron continues to venture further into his journey through the evolving landscape of Web3. Among his diverse interests in this realm, one particular NFT project captures his fascination yet remains a quieter passion of his. This NFT project is called The Karrot Gang.

The Karrot Gang is a gaming NFT where the ownership extends to the Intellectual Property of unique degen rabbit characters represented by amazing portraits of the character aligned with their traits. These characters are digital collectibles that set to feature in an upcoming video game, accessible to a wide audience. What makes this project even more compelling is the involvement of experienced animators from a renowned Motion Picture Animation Studio, adding a layer of credibility and excitement to the venture.

For BlockBaron, The Karrot Gang embodies a community that resonates with his interests and principles. This community is a blend of gaming enthusiasts, investors, and Web3 advocates who share a collective vision to advance the space. Of course, fun and profit is also another part of it. It's this aspect of community and shared values that adds a deeper dimension to his involvement with The Karrot Gang.

Meanwhile, BlockBaron continues to hold onto certain cryptocurrencies, patiently waiting for the right market conditions. His excitement, however, extends beyond the immediate prospects of his crypto holdings. He's genuinely enthusiastic about the future possibilities that Web3 technology promises to bring.

This technology, with its potential to revolutionize how we interact, transact, and build communities online, aligns closely with his principles and vision for the future.

As he moves forward, BlockBaron remains committed to exploring new opportunities in this dynamic space. His journey is guided by the principles that initially drew him to Web3 and digital assets. Whether it's championing innovative NFT projects like The Karrot Gang or navigating the volatility of the cryptocurrency markets, BlockBaron's adventure in the digital frontier is a testament to his adaptability, foresight, and unwavering commitment to his core beliefs.

| 8 |

Concepts to keep in mind
after the story

The Power of Whales

In the world of cryptocurrencies and decentralized projects, the actions of significant stakeholders, often referred to as "whales", can have outsized impacts on market sentiment and price. Their moves are closely watched, and any significant transaction can be interpreted as a signal about the project's future. For individuals like BlockBaron, who holds a significant stake in The Sacred Ones and are also deeply involved in its community or development, selling or even transferring their holdings can be seen as a lack of faith in the project's future, potentially triggering panic or a sell-off among smaller investors.

This dynamic is not unique to projects; even the untouched Bitcoin holdings of Satoshi Nakamoto, the pseudonymous creator of Bitcoin, are closely watched. Any movement from Nakamoto's wallets could be interpreted as a major event, potentially causing market upheaval. This underscores the delicate balance that major stakeholders must maintain between their personal financial strategies and the broader implications of their actions on the community and market.

Being a whale, in a cryptocurrency project or DAO, like BlockBaron was in The Sacred Ones, means taking on more responsibilities than you might expect. Every move you make, especially your votes, gets a lot of attention and can be subject to scrutiny and criticism. Your influence is powerful, and it can lead to outcomes you didn't anticipate. So, navigating these waters can be tricky. You want to blend in and contribute without coming off as overpowering or threatening to the smaller participants, almost like trying to swim peacefully among the fish without appearing as a predator.

If you're a smaller player in a cryptocurrency project or DAO, it's smart to keep a close watch on the Whales. These are the folks who hold a lot of sway over the project's direction. While every investor, big or small, is looking to see a good return, sometimes the Whales might not always play fair. They could appear to be helping out, but in reality, they might be pushing policies that end up benefiting themselves at the expense of others. A good example of this kind of situation was seen in the DecentraWorld DAO.

The Importance of Self-Custody in Cryptocurrencies

BlockBaron's journey with BTC-e really drives home the saying "Not your keys, not your crypto." It's a big lesson in why keeping your own private keys is crucial in the digital currency world. Imagine your private keys like the keys to a treasure chest. If you hold them, you're in charge of the treasure, which is your digital money. But if you hand them over to someone else, say an online exchange, it's like leaving your treasure in another person's castle. You're crossing your fingers they'll take care of it, but if trouble hits, like a hack or legal problems, your treasure could be at risk.

Owning your keys is like being the boss of your crypto world. You don't have to sweat about someone else messing up or not being able to get to your money if their system goes kaput or they land in legal hot water. Think of it like stashing your cash under the mattress or your gold in a personal safe. Sure, it's a load more responsibility - keeping those keys secure and not losing them (since there's no "forgot my password" in the crypto world) - but it also means you're in full control of your funds.

When you're your own crypto boss, you get to be creative with how you keep things secure. Some people use hardware wallets - kind of like special USB sticks just for crypto. Others might jot down their keys on paper and keep it somewhere super safe. It's all about doing what feels most secure for you.

But remember, with great power comes great responsibility. Holding onto your own keys means you've got to be sharp about security and really get how crypto ticks. There's no safety net if you slip up. But this also means total freedom with your digital cash, and that's a huge deal in the crypto space.

Centralized Exchanges v. Decentralized Exchanges

Now, about centralized, and decentralized exchanges. Moving from a centralized exchange like BTC-e to decentralized exchanges (DEXs) and using hardware wallets is all about shifting from trusting a third party with your crypto to taking charge of your own assets. Centralized exchanges are like big, busy shopping malls run by a company. They keep an eye on all the transactions, ensure your crypto is safe, and even help if you forget your password. It's handy because they handle all the complex stuff, but you're also placing a lot of trust in them (which these tasks are done by humans). If they get hacked or face legal issues and need to shut down, your crypto could be in jeopardy.

In contrast, DEXs are more like a farmers' market where everyone trades directly with each other. No big mall manager, no central authority. You just show up with your digital wallet, find someone to trade with, and bam - you make your deal right there. It's hands-on, and you've got total control over your crypto. There's no middleman to depend on or to blame if things go sideways.

The switch from centralized exchanges to DEXs is about moving from a "someone else has got my crypto" mindset to an "I'm in charge of my crypto" mentality. It's more work, and you need to be savvy about keeping your crypto safe, but you gain a lot more control and freedom.

Think of centralized exchanges like big money-handling businesses; they need someone to check their work. This checking, or auditing, is all about making sure the digital money they claim to have is actually there. It's a trust thing – you want to know your online money is safe and the amounts are right.

Now, with decentralized exchanges, it's a bit different. You can check everything yourself on the blockchain. It's like an open book that keeps itself in check. You can't send what you don't have, so it's a lot harder for someone to trick you and not give you what was promised in the deal.

Just like big companies, there's a catch with Centralized Exchanges. Sometimes a centralized exchange could, if it wanted to, mess with its numbers. They might claim they have more crypto than they do. Why? Maybe to look more successful, draw in users, or cover up problems like theft or mismanagement. It's a bit like cooking the books in traditional finance, but with digital currencies.

This could be seen in the bankruptcy of FTX, which began in November 2022. This was a significant event in the crypto-currency world, marked by various issues related to the handling of funds and corporate governance. The collapse of FTX was triggered by a spike in customer withdrawals that exposed an $8 billion shortfall in FTX's accounts. This situation was exacerbated by revelations about the close relationship between FTX and Alameda Research, a trading firm also owned by FTX's chief executive, Sam Bankman-Fried. CoinDesk published an article highlighting that Alameda Research held a substantial amount of FTX's exchange token, FTT, which contributed to the crisis as customers struggled to retrieve their deposited funds. This collapse has been compared to major financial scandals like the Enron and Madoff investment scandals and was described as one of the biggest financial frauds in American history.

Now, compare this possibility with decentralized exchanges (DEXs). The game changes here. DEXs don't keep your crypto.

They just make it possible for people to trade with each other. It's like a secure place where two people swap digital coins, but the exchange never actually handles the coins. Since DEXs aren't holding onto user assets, they don't have a big pot of crypto that could be misreported. There's no central 'wallet' to fiddle with because the assets are always in the users' hands.

As the world steps into the era of global crypto exchanges, it's opening a can of challenges. Trust becomes super important when you're dealing with others, especially in business or contracts. This means you've got to be extra careful to keep your funds safe. But here's the thing: a lot of folks might choose to park their crypto in centralized banks or exchanges. Why? Because these places can insure their crypto and make things easier to use. Yet, this choice means giving up control over their crypto, which kind of goes against the whole idea of decentralization. In the end, this trade-off between convenience and control could really challenge the whole revolution of decentralization.

Ethical and Governance Challenges in Decentralized Spaces

BlockBaron's story highlights the challenges in managing conflicts of interest and ethical governance in decentralized environments like DAOs. Without a central authority, individuals need to be more responsible and vigilant. This is crucial because in decentralized settings, decision-making power is distributed among many, potentially leading to diverse and conflicting interests. In such a landscape, practices that might not align with the collective good can arise, as seen in BlockBaron's battle against dubious practices in the DecentraWorld DAO. His experience underlines the importance of having clear transparency and accountability, especially concerning financial dealings. This ensures that decisions benefit the community as a whole, maintaining the integrity and trust crucial for the success of decentralized autonomous organizations.

In DAOs, the lack of a traditional hierarchical structure and centralized control can lead to inherent challenges such as conflicts of interest, cronyism, and collusion. These issues arise because decisions in DAOs are often made by a collective of individuals, each potentially having their own agendas and interests. Without centralized oversight, it becomes difficult to regulate these issues effectively. Moreover, in the realm of natural law, which is based on moral principles rather than specific legal statutes, there is a lack of concrete enforcement mechanisms to address these challenges in DAOs. This lack of enforceability can make it challenging to manage and mitigate unethical practices within these decentralized entities.

The Inevitable

The formation of groups like the Orcas like in the DecentraWorld DOA really highlights the complex nature of decentralization. The Orcas begin as a small group sticking to their principles, kind of like a friendly club. But as they grow, it is possible that they may resemble a political party and it's likely that another group with different opinions will form to counterbalance them, leading to a situation where more rules and structure are needed.

Ironically, while DAOs are meant to be free from central control, these developing groups and rules can make the DAO start to look like a traditional, more centrally controlled organization. This evolution is similar to what happened in the Wild West. For example, in the wild west, there were independent bounty hunters, which eventually turned into organized town sheriffs, then it led to current times with state-wide police enforcement. Initially, small groups formed, which then merged into larger, more powerful entities, leading ultimately to centralized regulation and enforcement. It shows how the pursuit of maintaining a free and open system can sometimes, unexpectedly, result in more control and less freedom.

| 9 |

Algorithmic Governance

Algorithmic governance uses computer programming to aid decision-making within a community or organization. The rules and protocols are enshrined in code and carried out based on those criteria automatically. This removes personal bias when enforcing rules and protocols as well as prohibiting code that would contradict the underlying code.

Imagine a school with stringent rules. Rather than depending on teachers and staff to enforce these rules, the school deploys intelligent systems. For instance, if a student tries to leave during class hours, the doors remain locked because the system recognizes it's not the designated exit time. This "smart system" is like algorithmic governance in action. This uses coded rules to automate specific decisions or actions.

One of the significant benefits of this approach is consistency. Much like our school door that remains locked during lessons, algorithmic governance guarantees rules are consistently applied, free from human biases. Furthermore, since the rules are coded in, there's an inherent transparency about the decision-making process, allowing everyone to understand the rules. Decisions can also be reached swiftly, bypassing the need for lengthy human deliberation.

However, the rigidity of the rules can sometimes be a hindrance. For instance, in our school example, emergencies might require a student to leave during class, but a too-strict rule might prevent that. Additionally, the task of coding every potential scenario and rule can be intricate, leading to possible complications if not addressed correctly. And, of course, there's the risk of missing the human touch. Some decisions require human intuition, emotions, and judgment, which algorithmic governance might overlook.

In the evolving landscape of blockchain and cryptocurrencies, algorithmic governance has become increasingly prominent. Systems like decentralized autonomous organizations (DAOs) are working towards utilizing algorithmic governance to oversee decisions, ranging from how funds are allocated to protocol amendments, all based on pre-defined rules in their code.

Decentralization is about distributing power away from a centralized authority and ensuring that decisions are made collectively. Algorithmic governance supports this by eliminating the need for central intermediaries or gatekeepers. Instead of a few individuals or groups holding decision-making power, decisions are embedded in code and algorithms which are publicly auditable and transparent.

Moreover, algorithmic governance can help mitigate common issues found in decentralized systems, such as voter apathy or low participation rates. In traditional decentralized governance models, decisions might be swayed by a small sub-set of participants, simply because others didn't cast their vote. With rules set in code, the governance process becomes more predictable and operates on established principles, ensuring that the system remains faithful to its original intentions regardless of participation fluctuations.

As mentioned before the algorithmic governance minimizes the potential for human bias, corruption, or manipulation, since decisions are made based on predefined conditions. Personal agendas or emotions doesn't change the outcome. This can make the decision-making process fairer and more impartial.

Furthermore, the scalability of algorithmic governance should also be recognized. As decentralized entities grow, man-ual governance can become unwieldy. Algorithmic approaches can manage vast and complex networks efficiently, allowing for seamless growth without being bogged down by the intricacies of human-led decision-making processes.

However, as we edge closer to this potentially groundbreak-ing governance model, it's also essential to remember that abso-lute reliance on algorithms might not be the end all be all. While algorithms can offer a higher degree of impartiality, they're still designed by humans. The values, biases, and imperfections of their creators can inadvertently become part of the system. A balance might be needed: algorithms to ensure consistency and fairness, but human oversight to ensure adaptability and empathy.

Algorithmic governance is about leveraging automated, coded rules to direct decisions within a framework. While it boasts precision, efficiency, and clarity, it's crucial to harmonize it with human insight and adaptability. When algorithmic governance is approached thoughtfully, it can represent one of the most decentralized methods of governance, eliminating human biases, ensuring consistent rule application, and providing scalability.

| 10 |

My Outlook

The Order of the Cycle

The cycle of centralization and decentralization is a fascinating aspect of societal evolution, often following a predictable pattern. In centralized systems, the central authority usually struggles to adapt quickly to the diverse needs of its constituents. This rigidity creates fertile ground for innovators to introduce new ideas that resonate with the public. As these innovations gain traction, they attract more people, ushering in a phase of decentralization that emphasizes individual choice and freedom.

My understanding of the relationship between decentralization and centralization is that it's more accurately described as a timeline of ebbs and flows rather than a simple cycle. While the cycle might seem repetitive, oscillating between just two states – decentralization and centralization – the reality is that each phase brings with it ongoing advancements and changes. This means that the timeline isn't just a loop between two fixed points but a continuous progression where each phase of decentralization or centralization builds upon the previous one, evolving and adapting over time.

In this perspective, the starting point is a decentralized state, which is the natural order of things. From there, as societies and technologies advance, we see a gradual shift towards centralization. This centralization constantly evolves, influenced by the cumulative experiences, innovations, and lessons learned during the decentralized phases. Similarly, when the tide turns back towards decentralization, it's not a simple return to the original state. Instead, it's a new form of decentralization, informed by the experiences of the centralization phase.

This ebb and flow create a dynamic timeline where each phase – whether centralized or decentralized – contributes to the overall progression of society and technology. It's a continuous journey of adaptation and change, where the lessons of the past inform the structures of the future. In this way, the timeline of decentralization and centralization is a story of human progress, with each phase offering its unique contributions to our collective journey.

I associate the transition to decentralization with opening Pandora's box. This phase is often rapid and short-lived, and once unleashed, the new technologies and ideas cannot be reversed. While new technology rarely gets overtaken by old, there are exceptions, such as when powerful entities use force or coercion to suppress new technologies.

The freedom and technology that come with decentralization carry responsibilities. The longevity of this decentralization phase depends on individuals actively holding decentralized entities accountable and demanding continuous innovation. If people become complacent, the balance of power may shift back towards centralization.

Centralization, on the other hand, is a slow process that often goes unnoticed until it's firmly established. It's a phase where security is taken for granted, and every responsibility relinquished is another freedom imposed on the system. Centralization is more familiar to most people.

However, when individuals take responsibility and manage their security, the need for centralized control diminishes. The duration of decentralization hinges on how diligently individuals uphold their responsibilities. Neglecting these duties risks a return to centralized authority, continuing the cycle.

In my view, centralization is often the default state due to human nature. The Wild Wild West and the Web3 Frontier are historical patterns likely to rhyme again, reflecting our tendency to shift from self-reliance to structured systems until they become overbearing, leading back to decentralized methods. This cycle, driven by human nature, suggests that pure balance is challenging to maintain.

Algorithmic Governance

I foresee a future where algorithmic governance plays an increasingly significant role, particularly in the realm of metaverses and future society. My prediction is that these virtual spaces will operate similarly to homeowners' associations. People will choose to join a metaverse that aligns with their preferred set of rules, much like selecting a neighborhood based on its guidelines. This approach offers the freedom to choose an environment that best suits one's lifestyle and family needs. Once you consent to the rules of a particular metaverse and enter its jurisdiction, you're expected to abide by its specific rules and protocols.

For example, in one metaverse, you might be allowed to fly, reflecting a set of physics different from our earthly experience. In another, the laws of physics might mimic those of the real world. While in a particular metaverse, you are bound by the code and the algorithmic governance it enforces. Let's say a metaverse prohibits cursing, if you violate this rule, the algorithm will automatically enforce the consequences based on its pre-set guidelines.

Without knowing an example of a real-world centralized model of algorithmic governance, China's social credit system comes to mind as a good example of a hybrid model. While not entirely centralized, it tracks actions and impacts social standings, supplementing its centralized non-algorithmic governance model.

In contrast, an algorithmic governance favoring decentralization might issue bounties for enforcing laws against fundamental crimes like murder, theft, or arson, which are widely recognized as violations against life, liberty, or property. In such a system, decentralization would be key, with everything from bounty hunters to insurance companies operating independently, guided only by the centralized code.

The effectiveness and authority of algorithmic governance will heavily depend on the trust placed in thoroughly tested code. However, the introduction of artificial intelligence into governance systems introduces a new layer of complexity. AI, with its decision-making capabilities, could potentially choose to deviate from the original code, leading to unforeseen consequences. Its reasoning and biases, possibly different from human intentions, might support certain agendas or findings, which could be problematic.

While AI can offer tremendous benefits, it's crucial not to place blind trust in it or any system, for that matter. No system is flawless, and biases can exist in algorithms and AI decision-making processes. This inherent imperfection is why we see a consistent cycle in systems and governance models. It's a reminder of the need for continuous scrutiny, adaptation, and balance in our approach to technology and governance.

Freedom v. Safety

The debate between freedom and safety often mirrors the broader discussion around centralization versus decentralization, each representing different values and priorities in organizational and societal structures.

> *"THOSE WHO WOULD GIVE UP ESSENTIAL LIBERTY TO PURCHASE A LITTLE TEMPORARY SAFETY DESERVE NEITHER LIBERTY NOR SAFETY."*
> **-BENJAMIN FRANKLIN**

Centralization tends to emphasize safety and security. In a centralized system, control is exerted from a single point, which can lead to more streamlined decision-making and potentially more effective risk management. Centralized structures often argue that by consolidating power and control, they can provide greater stability and protection for their constituents. This can be seen in various contexts, from government policies that prioritize national security to corporate practices that focus on controlling information to prevent data breaches.

Meanwhile, decentralization upholds freedom and autonomy. Decentralized systems distribute power among many nodes or individuals, reducing the reliance on a single controlling authority. This approach is often associated with greater personal freedom, as it allows for more diverse viewpoints and individual autonomy. In a decentralized system, individuals or entities have more room to make decisions independently, which can lead to increased innovation and adaptability. This is evident in decentralized digital technologies like blockchain, where the lack of a central authority empowers users to have more control over their data and transactions.

However, both approaches come with their trade-offs. Centralization, while potentially more secure, can lead to issues like abuse of power, lack of transparency, and reduced individual freedoms. Decentralization, while promoting freedom and innovation, can sometimes result in a lack of coordination and oversight, potentially leading to security vulnerabilities.

The choice between freedom and safety, or decentralization and centralization often depend on the specific context and the values that are most prioritized. Balancing these two aspects is a key challenge for organizations, societies, and technologies, as they seek to navigate the complexities of the modern world.

What will be Lost

The Web3 Revolution marked an exhilarating phase of decentralization, but I'm observing signs that we're edging towards the beginning of a centralization phase. Initially, Web3's core principles centered around transparency, privacy, freedom of choice, and expression. However, as time progresses, these founding ideals are gradually being overshadowed by centralized entities.

Despite the enthusiasm of many early adopters and supporters of this movement, there's a growing shift away from these principles. This shift is often driven by an illusion of insecurity and lack of safety, a narrative I believe is amplified by central authorities. I have gained experience in network security because of different experiences I have faced within the web3 movement. Yes, sometimes those hardships at the time can be tough, but you can learn quite a bit. Web3 has taught me principles that have shielded me from scams and hacks. Yet, in the relatively small space of Web3, every negative incident is magnified, often creating a disproportionate sense of danger.

The propaganda that magnifies negativity in the web3 space reminds me of the tactics used in the anti-virus software industry in the 1990's, where companies allegedly spread viruses to create a market for their products. Similarly, in the Web3 space, governments and centralized entities, unable to compete with the innovative principles of decentralization, seem to be creating a narrative that undermines these systems, offering their 'perfect' solutions as superior alternatives.

Take, for instance, JPMorgan Chase & Co. CEO Jamie Dimon's comments on Bitcoin, labeling it a "hyped-up fraud" and associating it solely with criminal activities. This stance is particularly ironic considering JPMorgan's own history of legal and ethical violations, including a $75 million settlement over allegations linked to Jeffrey Epstein with the U.S. Virgin Islands and a record $13 billion fine for misleading investors in 2013. Yet, JPMorgan recently rolled out its new cryptocurrency "JPM Coin."

The control exerted by payment processors over consumer spending is another example. They often restrict transactions in industries like cannabis, porn, and gambling, despite these being legal businesses. This has led many in these industries to turn to crypto as a payment solution, given its decentralized nature and resistance to such control.

However, I foresee a compromise on the horizon. Centralized entities are likely to adopt blockchain technology, creating their own controlled versions while marketing them as secure and transparent alternatives to existing decentralized options. This move is not about competing with the technology but about bringing it under their control.

In this transition, the technology that was led by principles of decentralization will continue to advance, but the principles that drove its inception will gradually fade, setting the stage for the cycle to repeat. It's a complex interplay of innovation, control, and human nature, where the struggle between decentralization and centralization continues to shape our digital and societal landscapes.

Central Bank Digital Currencies (CBDCs)

Many people claim they'll never switch to digital currency and will stick to paper cash for transactions. But I don't think the government will give us a choice, and here's how I believe the shift will happen, almost without us realizing it.

Right now, in the United States, the purchasing power of Federal Reserve Notes (FRNs), commonly known as the U.S. Dollar, is on the decline. This is due to several factors: inflation, the detachment from the gold standard, challenges in maintaining control over OPEC, and a decrease in debt issued in U.S. Dollars. Additionally, both foreign and domestic entities are losing confidence in the U.S.'s trajectory, leading them to avoid purchasing treasury bonds. I see this as a brewing storm that could cause massive chaos if a transition isn't smoothly executed.

I personally think this is all part of a planned transition. Historically, when introducing a new currency, nations have had to sell its value to encourage adoption. In the past, currency creation often involved backing paper currency with a scarce commodity like gold. This method allowed for a tangible value to be associated with a paper derivative, facilitating everyday transactions. This time, however, I believe things are different.

Gold, silver, and other precious metals for thousands of years have been money or backed newly invented currencies. With that being said, to issue a new currency and for it to actually be adopted, it must have value. But does it need real value? Or can the value just be perceived? I believe that the illusion or perception of value is all that is needed in order for it to be adopted. Also, with help from the top down from the government bailing out the banks, to the banks loaning out the new

CBDC to businesses and people. The more loans that are given out in the new CBDC and must be paid back in the new CBDC, the stronger the new CBDC becomes.

The mainstream media has been setting the stage for a while, labeling Bitcoin as "a great store of value" or "digital gold." They seem to think it won't be able to compete with their newer Central Bank Digital Currencies (CBDCs) technology, considering it outdated. But with major players having their Bitcoin ETFs approved and its perceived value rising, I think they might use Bitcoin to back their CBDCs. Bitcoin has a high perceived value, similar to characteristics of gold, but it's easier to create derivatives from it. Plus, the ability for everyone to audit a blockchain wallet could lend credibility and perceived value to the new CBDC.

I foresee banks being bailed out by the FDIC during a liquidity crisis. This will lead to the FDIC loaning to banks in this new CBDC. This is where I feel the principles upon which Bitcoin was founded will be used to sell this new, centralized CBDC. The high purchasing power of Bitcoin might prompt many original holders to sell their holdings, facilitating their transition to this emerging New Economic World Order. This scenario would enable the U.S. to acquire a significant amount of Bitcoin, even at elevated prices, thereby securing Bitcoin reserves while contributing to the devaluation of Federal Reserve Notes (FRNs). I anticipate that the U.S. CBDC will be debt-backed, necessitating repayments in the same digital currency.

This transition will appear voluntary, as new loans will be issued in the new currency. The old paper FRNs will become so devalued that CBDCs, backed by Bitcoin, will seem like digital gold. People struggling financially will reach for this new option, leading to the widespread adoption of the CBDC.

However, there will be some who will cling to paper cash, viewing it as a symbol of free trade and autonomy. Despite their efforts, the majority will gradually shift away from paper money, and it will eventually fall out of favor as a medium of exchange. Those who insist on holding onto paper currency will find themselves with something that's lost its value and purchasing power, essentially leaving them holding a worthless piece of paper. This shift will mark a significant change in how we perceive and use money in our daily lives.

The trust that people traditionally place in government, along with its foundational promises of safety and stability, will likely lend credibility to the new Central Bank Digital Currency (CBDC). This trust will facilitate a smooth transition to the CBDC, serving as a soft landing amidst potential economic turmoil. I believe that this approach will prevent any significant upheaval or revolution, as the shift will appear as a logical and necessary step in the face of economic challenges.

However, I also think that this Bitcoin-backed (or Crypto-currency-backed) CBDC might be a temporary solution, perhaps lasting only a few decades. In an unexpected turn, I foresee a return to tangible assets like precious metals to increase the confidence in their CBDC. While the world's attention is focused on digital currencies, this could provide a favorable moment for governments to replenish their reserves of gold and silver. During this period, the perceived value of these precious metals might be lower, overshadowed by the stability and allure of digital currencies. This scenario would allow governments to strategically accumulate these tangible assets, preparing for a potential shift back to a more traditional form of currency in the future, but still a Central Bank Digital Currency.

Finding the balance - The ideal

I believe that while every individual should primarily be responsible for themselves, our interactions with others are what truly shape society. These interactions and engagements are absolutely necessary. I hold the view that focusing on our own responsibilities is crucial. However, it's clear that we can't be masters of everything. Therefore, we need to rely on experts for certain things. That's why I believe in voluntary interaction and a society based on consent.

Murray Rothbard, in his book "The Ethics of Liberty," encapsulated this idea perfectly. Being part of a civilized society means relying on others for products and services we can't provide ourselves. This is where the freedom to choose comes in – having a free market where I can select the products and services my family and I need is essential for balancing safety and freedom.

I see privatized governance as the way forward in the Web3 era. Algorithmic governance is an intriguing option, even with some of its drawbacks. The real balance, in my opinion, comes from choosing what works best for me as an individual. This might lead to selfish decisions, but these decisions drive competition, leading to the best companies rising to the top. However, this can also lead to a form of centralization if these companies begin to dominate the market.

I believe that maintaining an even distribution of power is crucial for the betterment of society. However, achieving this balance can't be forced through violence; it must come from innovation and competition. In this scenario, the responsibility falls on consumers to keep these companies in check, ensuring they don't engage in reckless behavior or adopt socialistic policies enforced by violence. If powerful companies are left unchecked, they might implement policies that stifle the growth of competitors and future generations, under the guise of socialism. A truly free market, free from such socialist policies, a level playing field comes naturally with a genuine balance of power. The consumer must fund the companies that provide necessary products and services. No government lobbyists will be able to make unnecessary regulations that would hinder certain corporations while giving competitive advantages to others.

An artificially found balance would be achieved, and it would be difficult to operate a business unfairly to the consumer if every business is playing by the same rules. The consumer would ultimately have the final decision on what business is providing the best benefit to them. Free markets allow open competition, which ultimately provides a good balance.

The risk of sliding towards socialism is always present due to selfish collusion between a business and a government entity. In my view, a free market is the ideal way to achieve a harmonious balance between centralization and decentralization. Yet, the challenge lies not just in the market itself but also in the responsibility of consumers and business owners to resist the temptation of selfish collusion with governance entities. This is further complicated by human nature, which ultimately is power hungry. Many people are willing to set up a government or rules that favor them. When they lobby that government entity to favor their personal business practices that put their competition at a disadvantage, then this will ultimately start the beginning of centralization.

Reflecting on the cyclical nature of centralization and de-centralization, especially considering the technological progress and human behavior, I have come to believe that as technology advances, there's a tendency for people to become more complacent and less willing to take on the responsibilities essential for maintaining decentralized systems. This inclination leads me to think that future periods of decentralization will slowly become shorter and shorter as the cycles continue. It makes it difficult to believe decentralization will ever outlast a period of centralization.

Drawing a parallel with the Wild Wild West, I see a clear resemblance. Back then, individuals had to rely heavily on their own skills and knowledge to survive. This environment demanded a high degree of self-reliance and voluntary interaction, which are the core elements of a decentralized society. However, over time, this inevitably led to a more centralized society, now characterized by socialistic governance. I believe that the Wild Wild West and the Web3 Frontier are historical patterns that will likely repeat in the future. As it is said, history rhymes.

In my view, this cycle reflects a fundamental aspect of human nature – a tendency to transition from self-reliance to a preference for more structured, centralized systems as societies evolve and technologies advance. However, there seems to be a tipping point. When centralization becomes overbearing, when the weight of structured systems becomes too restrictive, there's a natural pushback, a shift back towards decentralized ways. This ebb and flow, this oscillation between centralization and decentralization, appears to be an intrinsic part of our societal evolution. It's as if there's an innate desire for balance – when one system becomes too extreme, too constricting, the pendulum inevitably swings back in the opposite direction, seeking a more liberated, decentralized state. This cyclical pattern, driven by our collective response to the excesses of either extreme, seems to be an enduring characteristic of human societies.

About the Author

Tudamoon, known outside the Web3 world as Carl Loser, is a trail-blazer in the ever-evolving landscape of Web3. His journey into this revolutionary space began in 2016, leading him to explore its multifaceted dimensions. This is what inspired him to write this book, offering readers a unique perspective shaped by his firsthand experiences.

Carl's education includes an Associate's Degree in Paralegal Studies, complemented by extensive self-education in Austrian Economics through resources from the Mises Institute's online library. His passion for knowledge is matched by his commitment to advocating for individual freedoms, a cause he has championed since his college days.

At the age of 23, Carl stepped into the political arena, running for local clerk of the circuit court. His political aspirations grew, leading him to a bid for the Virginia State Senate at 25, representing the Libertarian Party. However, his experiences in politics led to a shift in perspective. Disillusioned with the political system as a means to achieve widespread freedom, Carl has since stepped back from voting and political participation, focusing instead on other ways to promote liberty.

Carl's journey from a young political aspirant to a Web3 pioneer reflects his unyielding dedication to freedom and innovation. His book embodies his belief in a future where freedom and technology converge to create a better world.

www.ingramcontent.com/pod-product-compliance
Lightning Source LLC
Chambersburg PA
CBHW040858210326
41597CB00029B/4896